TELEVISION: Eth

£1.95

"There are only three theaters (networks) for television. If they are interested in buying a cop show, then that is what you as a craftsman must do because that's what the buyer wants."   —Norman Lear

"Many people who 'never watch television' watch twenty hours a week."   —Alan Alda

"In watching TV everyone is reinforced in their same positions."   —William Link

"Television has an enormous effect in terms of shaping ideas, attitudes, and awarenesses."   —Delbert Mann

"I tell stories that reflect an affirmative view of mankind."
                                    —Earl Hamner

"Every show on the air is trying to say something. You have to if you take yourself seriously."
                                    —Frank Glicksman

"It is very difficult for me to divorce what I am as a person and what I feel as an adult in this society from my work."
                                    —Norman Lear

"It is obscene to present constant dramas that show the only way to solve a problem is by violence."
                                    —Nancy Malone

"I think there are a lot of people in the industry who would welcome intelligent, nonviolent comment about improvements."   —David Hartman

TELEVISION
Ethics for Hire?

ROBERT S. ALLEY

ABINGDON
Nashville

Television: Ethics for Hire?

Copyright © 1977 by Abingdon

Library of Congress Cataloging in Publication Data

Alley, Robert S. 1932-
  Television: ethics for hire?

  Bibliography: p. 190
  1. Television broadcasting—United States—Moral and religious aspects. I. Title.
PN1992.6.A4   175′.1   76-44840

ISBN 0-687-41215-3

Chapter 4, "Media Medicine and Morality," has appeared previously in *Television as a Cultural Force*, ed. Richard Adler (New York: Praeger, 1976), copyright © 1976 by Abingdon. Dialogue on pp. 140-41 is from *Maude* teleplay by Susan Harris, story by Austin and Irma Calish. Copyright © 1972 Tandem Productions, Inc. All rights reserved. Used by permission. Dialogue on pp. 71, 72 is from *Medical Story* copyright © 1975 by Columbia Pictures Television, a division of Columbia Pictures Industries, Inc. All rights reserved. Used by permission.

MANUFACTURED BY THE PARTHENON PRESS AT NASHVILLE, TENNESSEE, UNITED STATES OF AMERICA

To
Norma
For
Norma

Contents

Preface

Credit for assistance in a project of this nature is necessarily extensive. There have been dozens of persons who have contributed to the content of this study. In what follows I have singled out those individuals whose assistance has proved significant in unique and singular ways. But in so doing I would want to affirm genuine appreciation for an array of persons in the television industry who consistently honored requests for information and interviews. Many of these individuals are named in the notes related to specific quotations drawn from taped personal interviews held in the summer and fall of 1975.

Earl Hamner, creator of *The Waltons* and fellow alumnus of the University of Richmond, provided massive aid to a potential interviewer with few interviewees in Hollywood. His kindness and cooperation over long hours are here gratefully acknowledged. Martin Kasindorf, Los Angeles Bureau Chief for *Newsweek,* opened some important avenues for inquiry as did his colleague, a friend, Kenneth L. Woodward, a general editor of *Newsweek.* A most gracious David Hartman extended his assistance over several months. The Aspen Institute, through its Program on Communications and Society, provided a week of intensive discussion that added immensely to my information and insight. The assistant director, Richard Adler, was consistently encouraging and helpful. Norman Lear and Virginia Carter offered access to the operations of TAT Communications Company and kindly responded to numerous requests for information. Steven Scheuer, editor of *TV Key,* has demonstrated sustained interest and has supplied valuable insights. Many other individuals have contributed significant comments and time. Quotations without notation in the text come from taped interviews which this author held with over forty persons during 1975 and 1976. All of these are here gratefully acknowledged.

Executives of the three commercial networks were receptive to questions during a busy time in their schedules in the fall of 1975. Professional staff member Alan Pearce of the House Subcommittee on Communications was most responsive to requests for data.

Several colleagues at the University of Richmond, including the president, E. Bruce Heilman, and other friends provided assistance, comment, and/or critique over the past three years. Among those who extended help were John Miller, Martin Ryle, Randolph Walker, Frank Eakin, James Hall, Robison James, Charles Nunn, Irby Brown, Henry Stewart, and Charles Glassick. A word of particular thanks goes to Jane Crum who typed while listening. For other distinctive and important contributions I wish to thank William S. Griffith, Barbara Gray, William C. Smith, and my father, Reuben E. Alley. Of course, all those named herein bear no responsibility for the final product which carries the author's name.

The University of Richmond Faculty Research Committee provided substantial funding for travel and a special University Theme Year Committee awarded a grant for course development. Many of my students offered incentive and aided in clarity of definition. One entire class gave valuable criticism of portions of the manuscript for which I am most grateful.

Preface

My two sons advanced ideas and offered motivation. Bobby read the manuscript, supplying valuable critical comment, and Johnny assisted with advice and technical help. My wife, Norma, gave focus, determination, intense interest, and as always, love.

Introduction

If one is to compose a book on the subject of television it seems almost mandatory that he immerse himself in the facets of the medium which lie behind the living room experience. The accomplishment of such a task may, upon first blush, appear extremely difficult for one accustomed to library research. However, as I have pursued the necessary information, often feeling myself in the role of a journalist, over a period of twelve months, the problem has been not the paucity of materials, but the proper distillation of a vast amount of data amassed from a generally quite cooperative industry. At times it was necessary consciously to resist being sucked into the system as I made the rounds of the Los Angeles scene.

In the ranking mass medium, one of the areas little known by the public is the complex of producers and directors who people Hollywood and its environs. The movie capital has become the tube capital. Yet even with the massive output of pulp fan magazines and the ubiquitous *TV Guide,* the personalities behind the product are essentially anonymous. In the past the public responded knowingly to movie names like Zanuck, Warner, Hitchcock, and Rank. But the mention of Ackerman, Link, Leacock, Victor, Glicksman, and Hawkins hardly conjure images of glamour or recognition. If, however, names like *Bewitched, Columbo, Hawaii Five-O, Marcus Welby, Medical Center,* and *Little House on the Prairie* are attached as TV shows produced by the above-named men, recognition is immediate.

Cinema was, and generally remains for most people, larger than life. Not only the theater experience, but the magnitude of the screen tend to separate the production from the audience. And while the actors have been important traditionally, so have been writers, directors, and producers. As an example, many more people are aware that Michael Douglas, a star on *The Streets of San Francisco,* left that series after success as producer of *One Flew Over the Cuckoo's Nest* than are knowledgeable about the name of the producer of the TV series Douglas is now leaving.

Television in its present manifestation is clearly not theater in any traditional sense. While one should be cautious about ascribing independent qualities to a mechanical device, the current state of the electronic science provides an experience of familiarity enhanced by the home locus of the set. Even when the family was clumped silently around one small instrument, the best description was home entertainment. Today the proliferation of sets tends to extend familiarity since nearly every room may be furnished with TV. Thus there is no longer even a special "theater" setting in the home. Carson, Cronkite, and Cannon have become coextensive with family living.

Several months ago, while gathering impressions for this study, I was seated in the office of Earl Hamner, waiting for him to complete a conference. He suddenly appeared in the company of Richard Thomas (John-Boy) whom I had never met. My immediate feeling was one of acquaintance. As I was introduced, what went unverbalized was the sense that I required no introduction. We had already met! In contrast, seeing Richard Widmark on the same day at the Burbank Studios, I thought "movie star." People in the TV industry say this is a common reaction to actors in the medium. In a sense they are extensions of one's family experiences, and this kindles a felt kinship. Television viewers tend to identify with the fictional characters, whereas in movies it has been and remains far more common to identify the fictitious screen figure with John Wayne or Cary Grant or Robert Redford. If Alan Alda *is* Hawkeye and Bea Arthur *is* Maude, who were Wayne and Grant and Redford? Repetition of character portrayal over weeks, months, and years is a kind of saturated typecasting which is in marked contrast with the varied roles of movie stars, seldom seen more than once in a particular part. Movie comparisons are, therefore, difficult, and the public may find it wiser to consider TV a totally different enterprise which just happens to occupy the same space as the old movie studios.

In spite of its very personal nature, most people have only slight information about and acquaintance with the shapers and makers of television. And what there is, is usually restricted to glamour-oriented studio tours and fan magazines. In the world of politics the press compensates the public for its distance from the action by efforts at competent reporting. Unfortunately, this is not the case in TV entertainment. Alongside the "gossip" columnists in newspaper TV sections, there are a few legitimate critics, probably read by a small percentage of viewers and often reflecting a jaded sense of hopelessness at the mammoth job set before them—intelligently to assess seventy shows or more a week.

Likely the most influential instrument is *TV Guide.* Its quality is varied, with many articles puffing "stars," while discussing their idiosyncrasies that make them "just like us." Its covers are almost exclusively reserved for leading men and women. Its editorial stance is jaundiced, reflecting anger at Nixon's demise and seeing network news as a "liberal" demon. While there are some well-written articles by competent writers, *TV Guide* is largely a carrier of star tidbits, spiced with "up from the ranks" acting marvels with strange habits, albeit great "human beings." Finally, it is not news; it is a profiting portion of the industrial giant known as network television. In his provocative book *The Mind Managers*, Herbert Schiller comments, "Beholden to the corporate economy for its advertising revenues and free publicity, *TV Guide* repays its benefactors in full, as a marketing tool and as a 'neutral' informational source which is, in reality, partisan to the hilt."[1]

The sum of all that has been said is to affirm that at present the flow of information about network television is insufficient, given the significant position it occupies in home and family. This condition coupled with the intriguing nature of the television experience have been the two motivating forces in this present undertaking. I believe Americans need knowledge of such a close associate as TV has become to almost all of us. Some past efforts in this direction have been fruitful,[2] but by its nature TV is constantly changing and its ripple effects are enormous. It is to be hoped that this volume will offer some insight into the huge industry that supplies us all with familiar talking furniture.

The broader purpose is the examination of the character of the medium. Over the past several years professors have become aware of the fact that we are now, for the first time, instructing students reared on the tube. Their homes have been the traditional locus of moral instruction. No matter the underlying ethical assumptions of any particular family, moral direction was presumed to be the preserve of home and, by extension, the religious institution to which any given family adhered. Control over entry into the home lay, historically, with parents. Newspapers, books, magazines, and, consequently, ideas, were filtered through parental philosophy before becoming openly available to children. To be sure, this was not foolproof, but for generations children led protected lives. Public schools and the range of friends found there injected the only consistent outside influence not directly conditioned by parental intent. Radio began a change in this pattern, restricted though it was to audio alone. Now that television has become a total component of the home, parental control over movement of material into the family has been seriously eroded. Restricting the viewing habits of growing children becomes, year by year, ever more difficult.*

To complicate this picture, a style was set in the fifties with the early use of TV as a convenient baby-sitter, contributing thereby to surrogate parenthood in millions of homes. Further, the post–World War II phenomenon, the family room, allowed and encouraged compartmentalization in which leisure was separated from family life. Finally, in the fifties the TV set usually found residence in such rooms at a time when children were regularly sent to recreate alone, out of the way. Any figures on family viewing are suspect because this phenomenon was succeeded by the private possession of small sets by an even larger portion of the younger generation, particularly among the more affluent.

Hence, parents and children alike need to identify the soul of the entertainment that mightly joins what remains of the family circle. What are its moral assumptions? This need not be a defensive quest, having only the purposes of censorship or condemnation. Rather knowledge could facilitate understanding. In the process some pointed

*In the discussions that follow no effort has been made to define terms such as morality and ethics in a technical sense. In broad terms we are considering alternatives which provide human beings with guidance for the conduct of life. In that sense "moral" and "ethical" are often employed interchangeably.

queries should be posed. What has TV been saying? Have the producers and writers intended to say anything about values? Can any conclusions be drawn from a selected examination of medical shows, police drama, and comedies? Are there alternatives to the present TV diet? What has been the role of industry and government respecting TV programming? Answers to such diverse questions as these may provide a tentative agenda for assessment of America's recent past from a different perspective.

One of the presumed values of our cultures which is deeply embedded in most all traditions is the authority of the home. (An underlying assumption of this book is that such authority has eroded dramatically in the past two decades and that television has played a major role in that erosion.) Students who in the fifties and early sixties were adjusting their lives to accommodate rebellion against parents or home are now parents of boys and girls entering their teens. From observations concentrated upon late teens, it is my opinion that today's teens are just not interested in such questions as rebellion. Many youths easily affirm parental rights to hold "old" ideas, but are no longer torn by the belief that they must choose the same style or rebel. Church and home no longer claim with certainty those adolescents who once responded under compulsion. In the second decade of their lives many are seeing themselves as fulfilled and as free agents who respond to compassion and love, and in turn offer the same. But they reject the conclusion that such love dignifies a claim of ownership over a child's soul, his life. This might be understood in light of the horrendous mess into which today's adults have cast teen-agers. Political corruption and industrial crime are no longer withheld from view. TV has undermined our ability to mythologize our antics, to hide the truth. In short, TV has stripped us bare.

And where does this leave the teen-ager? He or she is more sophisticated, more informed than any comparable generation in history, and yet also more totally unprepared and vulnerable, rushing to adult decision making in cultures woefully unwilling to accept the new patterns and sentiments. Authority has diminished and TV has, I believe, played a major part in the revolution. And for that reason it is urgent that we all come to terms with our new companion. The last thing we dare is to fight with holding actions. News media bombard our youth with the information that marijuana is less harmful than cigarettes or alcohol, but our legislative system demands arrest of young persons for the least dangerous while collecting taxes on the other two. And what of youths reared to this heritage, fully conscious of its hypocrisy long before there is commensurate maturity to blend it to a useful life? To many, TV has told the truth while authority figures—parents, the law, the church—have veiled the truth. Little wonder TV assumes all too often the responsibility of alternative parent. It makes no demands and is, as we shall demonstrate, exceedingly tolerant of variant positions and ideas. We are discovering a truth long ignored in religion, that authority lies only where the person involved chooses to place it, not where the authority of dogma or parent would have it. What is not so clear is whether a culture can survive that type of freedom. It is certain that it cannot if it only cries "anarchy" when faced with the reality.

Perhaps what is being suggested is that the parents put aside their role as authority and seek to make sense to the child. Television may have aided in the creation of an environment in which children will listen, but they will not be told. For indeed, parents must make sense out of the world for themselves and then in conversation with their offspring. They must not become paranoid, nor allow the blue funk of the teen years to be translated into hopelessness. A recent article by Richard Hunt of Harvard struck my desk just as this chapter was being completed. He describes teaching a class on German history and how it responded to ethical questions. His remarks are pointed.

> Maybe in the end it is true that quite a number of students nowadays hold to a despairingly deterministic view of the past and present. Clearly some trends of our time seem to be running toward a no-fault guilt-free society. One might say the virtues of responsible choice, paying the penalty, taking the consequences all appear at low ebb today.
>
> Somehow I have got to convey the meaning of moral decisions and their relations to significant outcomes. Most important, I want to point out that single acts of individuals and strong stands of institutions at an early date do make a difference in the long run.[3]

The parent too must feel this pressure and react in rational ways to make the difference.

If TV has begun to usurp the parental role, then wherein may an intelligent response be found? Television has made it clear to all who would be realistic that the family must expand its vision, must open itself to new influences. This does not prejudge the end product; nor does it deny the necessity of suggesting alternative paths for TV. For a beginning, should television continue its commercial orientation toward mass audiences or examine the possibility of select publics, members of subgroups in the pervasive "over culture"? For twenty-five years Americans have depended upon polls, surveys, statistics, and graphs to inform about the tube. Research has tended to be restricted to laboratory investigations under controlled conditions. It seems time to call for a subjective look at TV with a concern for its humanistic characteristics. A chief value of TV lies in its potential for the artist to

19

communicate directly. Television may have many practical uses, but its primary character lies in two areas: as a conveyor of information and as an artistic medium, a maker as well as a reflector of cultures. A point of entry to a consideration of these areas is a brief historical look at the tube.

Chapter I
TV Morality: A Point of Entry

If the *New York Times* can be accepted as sufficient documentation, television celebrated its fiftieth anniversary in 1976.[1] On January 22, 1926, John L. Baird gave a practical demonstration to a London audience of living scenes "viewed the instant they took place." By October of that year Baird had received a license from the British Post Office for "radio-television transmission." By 1927 American Telephone and Telegraph provided a public display of two processes for transmitting pictures "live." One was the appearance of Herbert Hoover over a wire system from Washington to New York. The second, and far more revolutionary, was a wireless setup which transmitted a vaudeville act from Whippany, New Jersey, to New York City. Television criticism may have begun that year as observers began to comment upon the future of the new electronic device. In April of 1927 the *Times* commented that television "outruns the imagination of all the wizards of prophecy. It is one of the few things that Leonardo DaVinci, Roger Bacon, Jules Verne and other masters of forecasting failed to anticipate. Even interpreters of the Bible are having trouble in finding a passage which forecasts television. H. G. Wells did not rise to it in his earlier forecasting."[2]

Auspicious as its beginnings were, television languished while other means of mass communication flourished. It was in 1927 that Al Jolson helped establish "talkies" with *The Jazz Singer*. The movies conquered the sound barrier the same year that AT&T demonstrated the wireless from Whippany. Concurrently, in the year 1927,

"RCA organized NBC as two semi-independent [radio] networks," and within months CBS, with William Paley as president, was offering NBC competition.[3]

Although Baird could write in 1930, "Those who possess 'Televisors,' actually see the faces of the people who are being transmitted, and can watch their movements on a small screen. *So that television in the home has arrived*,"[4] the medium nevertheless failed to prosper, and in the United States the first license for a television station was not sought until the forties.

Meanwhile, radio grew rapidly from its crystal beginnings. Receivers became more sophisticated as did the variety of programming. Radio, unlike television, provided a wealth of imaginative ideas to two decades of Americans. Radio drama created in the listener the desire to participate by extending his auditory experience without limit. The unseen stark studios were in sharp contrast with the rich panorama of images conjured by adults and children alike in the long years of depression and war. Further, radio was a way of life for two generations of children, a way that evaporated by the mid-fifties as quickly as it had burst upon this nation in the thirties. To this day the introductory music and words of afternoon and evening radio drama can initiate a flood of memories distinct and different for each person. Experience of radio was far more demanding than television. But the dreams stimulated remained within the context of traditional family. Radio, further, was malleable, conforming to the hearer who gave it mobility. It stimulated laughter and conversation. Words bore significant freight.

The first flowering of television began in 1951, twenty-five years after Baird's demonstration. The year 1951 seems propitious since it was in that year that the transcontinental cable became operative. In those post–

World War II days George Schuster, president of Hunter College, offered an early challenge. He described television as an educational conundrum and warned "unless something is done about raising the level of television our cultures will become more and more immature and silly."[5] This 1950 admonition that anticipated the coming ubiquitous nature of the tube has been renewed many times. Since then, critical comments from the academic community have often decried the deleterious effects of television viewing upon the cultures. Rightfully concerned over quality and the preservation of cultural strength, professors have found little time for constructive criticism. Indeed, in the sixties, "intellectualism" was often equated with denial of ownership of a TV set. One is reminded of the snob appeal for the intellectual of owning a Volkswagen in the fifties. Spurred on by Newton Minow's "vast wasteland" remark the academic voice remained strident and negative. That may explain Martin Mayer's caustic observation, "The charge that television is intellectually inconsequent comes with ill grace from a literary and academic community that regards Norman Mailer as a genius and Marshall McLuhan as an insightful guide . . . a community that made *The Greening of America* the most talked-about book of its season."[6]

This lingering suspicion of TV is reflected on many campuses today. In a 1975 conference on television criticism held in Aspen, Colorado,[7] one participant noted that her interest in television criticism should be kept in confidence until she was granted academic tenure. While clearly meant in a humorous vein, the truth is that academics are often loathe to accept television research as scholarly unless it is done within the confines of the departments of psychology and sociology. It seems to be off limits for those who practice seriously the disciplines of literature, history, philosophy, and ethics.

The mass of materials presently available from social scientists on television and human behavior is staggering. The Rand Corporation recently issued a three-volume work entitled *Television and Human Behavior* which contains in its more than seven hundred pages "2,300 bibliographic citations, accompanied by brief descriptions of the contents." An examination of the Rand studies reveals that most research projects described were laboratory oriented with little or no regard for value content or for the role of the makers and movers of the industry of television. Muriel Cantor, in a fine book, suggests that "most researchers, when they consider media content and its effects, may see the audiences in social context but ignore the communicators and the social context in which they work."[8] Thus, while the social scientists may not necessarily be faulted for isolation from creative sources, it remains a wide-open field of inquiry.

Beyond the classroom and laboratory, television has spawned its supply of professional critics both national and local. The quality of these various efforts at criticism remind one of a 1959 remark by Hubbell Robinson, then executive vice-president at CBS, "Television desperately needs criticism. Whether it needs the kind of criticism it gets is something else again. The great majority of the bashes aimed against it are superficial, aimless, uninformed, distinguished by fury rather than fact."[9] David Littlejohn, a practicing critic and professor at the University of California, Berkeley, has posited the proposition that what is needed in the world of TV criticism are people who like the medium and in addition write clearly and have consciences. At present this is not a large company with names like John O'Connor, Steve Scheuer, John Leonard, and Les Brown prominent on a reasonably short list.

TV Morality: A Point of Entry

One of the persistent problems of the TV critic has proved to be the follow-up of series. Immediate, early reactions to network programs may affect the future of a given series, but if it does not, nothing further is likely to be written about a drama that may put in a weekly appearance over a period of many years. For instance, a careful search of the *New York Times* revealed not one single mention of the long-running *Ben Casey* from inception to cancellation. Norman Lear is fond of quoting critics who foresaw doom for *All in the Family* after one episode. The recently developed *Good Morning, America* on ABC was verbally blasted by at least two important critics within hours of the first showing. In fact, the critics appear to have assumed that the same techniques employed for drama criticism apply to TV. By the same token that TV is not theater, likewise is deserves different treatment from critics. It seems often that TV critics employ critical faculties effectively only after the death of a series, and postmortems count for little as an aid to viewer response.

And where are the historians, the philosophers, the ethicists, the literary scholars who frequent our halls of learning and turn attention to Watergate, Vietnam, Kurt Vonnegut, and James Dickey? The humanities have traditionally provided a platform for examination and critique of culture. The humanist is not restricted by the laboratory conditions that presumably hamper the social scientist, or by the fear of being co-opted that may trouble media critics in the press. The humanist can supply a needed overview of the TV industry that consumes our time and energy. He or she can speculate on the basis of content analysis, fully aware of the conflicting findings of colleagues in other disciplines, but able to venture beyond, to inquire into motive and purpose, and to weave some conclusions based thereupon.

As critics have exercised their craft since 1950, television has been the target for many quick shots. In the early days TV was attacked by one medical man who made direful predictions about children developing stunted feet from too little walking and from another who predicted malformed jaws in children from too much TV viewing on the floor. In more recent years TV has absorbed much blame for increased crime rates and sexual license. Some politicians have seen it as the cause of Richard Nixon's collapse. As has been noted earlier, *TV Guide* has, within the past eighteen months, launched a vigorous, unrelenting attack on television news as a cause of the decline of "right-leaning" politics. Physicians now fear that TV may damage eyes and, through radiation, shorten lives. At present the decline in Scholastic Aptitude Test (SAT) scores among high school students and the apparent inability of young men and women to write coherent sentences is being blamed, at least partially, upon the technological giant. [10]

The sum of the evidence and commonsense opinion leave little doubt that twenty-five years of television programming has affected nearly all aspects of America's multicultures. Statistics on viewing time alone are convincing on this score. In fact, TV has become a cultural phenomenon in its own right. One executive observed that TV may as often *be* the news as a report of news. The result has likely been the loss of some cherished and valued traditions of past cultures. Some things of worth will surely die as a result of TV. Similarly, the printing press undoubtedly caused a decline in the production of illuminated pages in manuscripts, thereby conceivably resulting in the loss of a distinct art form, but that same press helped create a cultural and intellectual revolution whose influences still excite historians. Likewise, in the twentieth century it would appear that humanists might bear heavy responsibility for alerting citizens to alternative patterns of living and learning made mandatory by scientific advance comparable to the Gutenberg era.

If, as some assert, TV contributed to civil unrest in the sixties, might those moments be viewed as creative, opening the entire range of American cultures to millions of adults and children, until then locked in the ghetto existence of metropolitan slums. As one observer notes, the electric plug is causing all hell to break loose.

There is no arguing that television is a monumental challenge, but it need not be characterized as a villain. And the challenge is to educators, politicians, and citizens, as well as to the TV industry. We must find the handle on the medium and seek new avenues to take advantage of twentieth-century inventive genius. Indeed, the present form of network monopoly is most probably transitory. TV executives preferring not to be quoted anticipate radical alteration in both patterns of viewing and programming in the next decade. Videodiscs, pay–cable TV, and public broadcasting are only a few of the threats to total network dominance in the last quarter of the century. It is this prospect of shifting control over TV to which our multicultures should turn their energies.

If, as some have charged, TV has adversely affected writing habits of our children, then it is the educators who must examine alternatives, for television is most assuredly not going away. Of course, everything, including present educational philosophy with its phonetic emphasis, affects writing. Radio, cinema, LP records, concerts, paperbacks, and the automobile all have a role to play in the development among teen-agers of the capacity to function in the traditional world of art and literature.

Electronic media are predictably working to unloose disruptive social and political ideas, along with new forms of sensibility and expression. . . . Meanwhile, the schools are still pushing the old technology; and, in fact, pushing it with almost hysterical vigor. Everyone's going to learn to read, even if we have to kill them to do it. It is as if the schools were the last bastion of the old culture, and if it has to go, why let's take as many down with us as we can.[11]

Paradoxically, at the same time that TV may be creating conditions for revolution, just because it has been locked to mass appeal and money-conscious advertisers, TV drama has not been on the forefront of any social upheavals. It probably has had, so far, about as much impact on the society as the "all man" father has upon a son whom the father wishes to be aggressive, fight back, and play football. Experience has shown that most such sons emerge into the world of adulthood as conformists, challenging nothing in the society, remaining fiercely loyal to old alma mater, and expressing violence only against a losing coach. Like the father, TV has been a conserver of traditional values, reinforcing a type of civic piety. The zenith of this piety is exhibited in the sports broadcaster and the flag-waving half time. Sports people live in the pollyanna world of make-believe and often equate it with some type of Americanism. We shall have reason to return to this theme in chapter 7.

It is this paradox that will be scrutinized in succeeding chapters. We are confronted with a phenomenon that shakes family tradition while at the same time regularly endorsing old-time virtues. This characteristic cannot be dismissed lightly, for it is this contradiction which offers interesting possibilities to a disturbed nation. As we shall see, within the limits imposed by a nervous bureaucracy, creativity emerges, prejudice is exposed, ideas are developed. It is doubtful that television ever was a "vast wasteland," but it appears today as a giant containing an array of creative talent frustrated but working.

Chapter II
The Tube: A Self-Image

When I undertook this investigation in the spring of 1973 the ramifications were not fully perceived. My initial concept was to establish categories and ascertain how various series on television might be making assumptions of an ethical nature in some or all the categories. The results of that research are now scattered through this volume after a more comprehensive examination of the medium. Meeting the persons who make the decisions in TV became a priority, and the result has proved a humanizing experience in which the activity behind the tube gained an invigorating dimension. What follows here are reflections upon interviews with several dozen individuals—network executives, producers, government officials, actors, and critics—as they discussed the elusive nature of values on prime-time television.

In Hollywood, the fifteen producers of currently successful television series whom I interviewed in 1975 and 1976 impressed me as intelligent, highly motivated individuals. They were diverse in interest, people who exhibited an intense commitment to a profession.[1]

The TV producer is a middleman, operating between the network and the actors, program practices, and writers. However, I must say, as a group, they tended to identify almost completely with the creative community on the West Coast. Of course, these producers have numerous considerations in mind when contemplating a series. The question I asked was whether they gave a degree of priority to moral or ethical content. Beyond that, the likelihood of effect on the viewing public was thoroughly explored. No matter how the question was answered, to a person, all affirmed some concern about the moral and ethical content.

Several producers seemed skeptical of ethical impact, while readily admitting the presence of moral statements in most all evening drama and comedy. One producer, Jim Brooks of *The Mary Tyler Moore Show*, was more cautious. Six years ago this series appeared asking whether a young woman who had enjoyed a mature relationship sexually, having broken the relationship, could "make it on her own." In the progress of the show the opening song has been altered to affirm that she "is going to make it after all." The primary thrust of MTM productions seems to be "that people should be open and loving toward one another, if that's possible." For Mary and her friends issues are secondary, says Brooks, because, "by what virtue are we experts on any issue there is? Except, we are experts on the people we write about." Yet, since he also feels that "everything we do is social comment," Brooks may be employing "issues" in specific relation to political matters.

In conversation Jim Brooks reveals himself as a striking combination of sincere commitment to craft and delight-fully humorous personality. He speaks admiringly of Norman Lear's achievements in setting new standards for comedy on television. By the same token, one can be equally appreciative of the "muted" tones of *Mary Tyler Moore*. For Brooks, "it's exciting when you can do a television show that flirts with the edges of art . . . especially in comedy." And he is particularly serious when he contends that "there is more good comedy being done on television than anywhere else."

Brooks's comments, considered as a whole, do imply major effect by television upon the culture. He is reticent to allow Mary to presume to "comment on issues"; yet she and the cast do take positions on women's rights, sex, impotence, homosexuality, smoking, planned parenthood, marriage, divorce, religion, the communications industry, and medicine. All these have received significant comment in the last six years. So even though it is "not our object to say anything" according to the producer, MTM speaks effectively to the society of the seventies.

Brooks is joined in his opinions at several significant points by two energetic and enthusiastic gentlemen, William Link and Richard Levinson. The two have been associated with a plethora of TV fare—*Columbo, Ellery Queen, That Certain Summer, The Gun.* Both men obviously enjoy conversing on the subject of TV values and have done so often. This made for a lively exchange when we talked at length amid the din of the Universal Studios commissary. Levinson, who tends to dominate in verbal response to questions, spoke thoughtfully about the medium and values.

> In our view no one can really measure how much power television has to teach and persuade. Obviously it can be enormously effective in the case of *Sesame Street*, news programming, or a series of documentaries, such as *Civilisation*. And Lord knows TV advertising literally lifts people from their chairs and sends them out to buy. But we wonder if a television drama of a polemical nature has any effect whatsoever on those who watch it. . . . We in dramatic television would be flattering ourselves out of all proportion if we began to feel that even at our most artful we could actually change social and political views.

They do admit that if you keep the polemic or message subtle and inobtrusive, more effect is felt. If we know we are watching a message, we may be put on guard.

No one whom I encountered in Hollywood impressed me more with their intelligence and breadth of knowledge. These were talented craftsmen, artists. And it was in that role they spoke of changing social views. In fact, in popular culture, the possibility of producing effect may not be at all dependent upon artistic gift. Thus, the idea of self-flattery is not at issue. These men are using a medium which is so very different from the theater that comparisons with the historical effect of art on society are not altogether helpful. It is doubtful that effect ceases when TV moves from news and advertisements to drama. It may be less obvious and hence more subjective. Pressed on this point Levinson did agree there might be created a "general ambiance over a period of time."

Moving to intention, the two men agreed that "no single piece of television, other than the commercials, is geared to sell an idea." Some of their professional colleagues tended to challenge this, and we shall have occasion to return to that theme frequently.

Nancy Malone, actress and now vice-president for TV comedy development for Twentieth Century-Fox, was one who demurred. Ms. Malone is impressive. Her art and thoughts seemed to fuse. "I want to be associated with and develop shows that have some kind of morality without a stamp, but something that says one can function with a certain amount of love and faith." She is convinced that all but the most callous industry people have value structures that affect their activities. A major participant in the production of *Jane Pittman*, Malone insists, "The work I will be involved in kind of comes out with my point of view injected into it in some manner, whether it be the focal point of the story or just a peripheral situation." Link and Levinson concur at this point, stating, "We could not write effectively about something we did not believe in."

Delbert Mann, an urbane and scholarly gentleman whose credits include *Marty* and *Omnibus* and the legendary *Heidi* insists that "television has an enormous effect in terms of shaping ideas, attitudes, and awarenesses." And a producer of *Police Story*, Stan Kallis, says, "We insist upon pressing for a moral point of view."

Two respected actors with whom I discussed these matters tended to support the idea of major influence exerted by TV. Both David Hartman and Alan Alda agreed with Mann and Kallis. Larry Gelbart, producer of *M.A.S.H.*, leaves the impression of concurring with Alda that *M.A.S.H.* "presents a very strong humanist point of view." Of TV drama and comedy Alda noted that "the message gets across in inverse proportion to its being made conscious," for "the unspoken assumptions are what mold the audience."

Curious to know what officials at the Federal Communications Commission might think about this subject, inquiry was made at the Washington headquarters. There was no doubt where they stood. One member of the FCC staff volunteered that Norman Lear was lowering the moral standards of Americans. One would have to search extensively to find a more vigorous claim for TV impact. Interestingly, Lear himself is inclined to reject "the thought that television has all that much effect." Yet he does say "it is not possible for me to make an audience laugh and separate that from the other parts of me that care about what's happening and my interest in people." And in the final analysis Lear does really expect results.

I wouldn't wish to do the show [*All in the Family*] if I didn't feel that the fact he's [Archie] a horse's ass for five years is going to be apparent because the average viewer has every bit as much sophistication as the average television producer on a gut level and he'll understand.

Twenty-five hundred miles away, responding to the same general line of questioning, quite different emphases emerged. Network executives at the top level reside in New York near the Rockefeller Center. Separated by the width of a continent from the creative community, but instantly connected via electronics, they are sequestered in glass towers within minutes of each other. Since the area of values so directly affects the persons in broadcast standards or program practices, vice-presidents responsible for program review were interviewed, leading to conversations with Herminio Traviesas of NBC, Tom Swafford then of CBS, and Al Schneider of ABC. Because of their function these individuals have not inappropriately been described as censors.

While the three men impart quite different impressions individually, they have a common cause, a belief in the wisdom of their position and responsibility. Editors employed by Swafford, making perhaps $16,000 per year, were "the most powerful persons at CBS because they can tell a Grant Tinker or Ford Motors, 'Not on this network!' "

Traviesas believes that the "country is still very basically puritanical," and he moves from that faith to affirm that "you cannot judge what the public will accept just because we live in very sophisticated New York or Los Angeles." He sees TV as having a determining influence and for that reason applies quite strict guidelines about matters as particular as the use of "hell" and "damn." In a major dramatic show you should "keep 'hell' and 'damn' out for the first fifteen minutes." Yet he resents those who "tend to give the public the belief that the decisions are made by some stupid man who doesn't like the word 'hell.' "

Traviesas is not stupid. He knows, in his mind, that he

loses money for sales. He also believes that his job requires him to defend the sensitivities of what one might describe as middle America from the sophisticated East. He feels the *Maude* abortion episodes were a mistake because abortion "is a very controversial subject." At the same time, he is a man concerned for women's rights and the rights of minorities.

Tom Swafford, until recently a CBS vice-president, is a man in motion. A recovered alcoholic, he exudes care about fellow human beings. While I was in his office last fall he spent an hour planning efforts to assist an alcoholic who had begun to drink again and was in danger of losing his job. As he talked about television, he phrased his position somewhat differently from Traviesas. For Swafford, the job was to protect the network, to give it time to mature. He accepts "the fact that CBS cannot be everything to everybody, if they are to avoid *Gentle Ben* and animal shows." He wanted to "engineer our way through the next few years." He has no doubt about TV impact and in that vein was "not trying to keep things off the air" but rather sought to discover "what should be on the air." I find Norman Lear's description of Swafford apt. He "is a very educated, sensitive gentleman in a most complicated job. . . . With his whole heart he agrees with me, but his position requires him to disagree."[2] The recent decision by CBS to replace Swafford removes a perceptive figure from the executive offices.

ABC's shop is guarded by a most businesslike, no-nonsense lawyer, Al Schneider. He can inform you quickly and precisely concerning his network.

We as a department are responsible for carrying out indirectly for the owned stations and for the affiliated stations and for the network the responsibility of a broadcaster to operate in the public interest, convenience, and necessity.

Schneider appears to pursue his task methodically with a firm resolve.

> I think that we have an obligation to be responsible in terms of what we show and what we reflect and what's happening. We also have a responsibility in terms of leading by inching ahead. And that is a way of reflecting too, because we are no different than literature, motion pictures, books, magazines, newspapers, except to the extent that we reach more people more of the time in their own home, free and by the purchase. To what degree does that now put different conditions upon what I am permitted to publish, in a sense, by my medium? It seems to me, in order to exist as a commercial broadcaster, the mandate quite properly is to attract most of the time most of the audience, but not to ignore the nation of minorities.

When asked what the network's place in the society might be, he replied that it was essentially to entertain and "not to do anything that is harmful." He does seem to feel the network has some responsibility to shape culture, but he wisely challenged any simple definition of what that might be.

William Link told me last summer that I had to show that television "does have influence, or you are not going to have a book." His colleague Levinson, in the same conversation said, "You don't have to have the answers, just raise the questions." I have no doubt that sufficient questions have been raised. I would suggest that the evidence adduced in this chapter is a preliminary response to Link's concern sufficient to lead us to a consideration of the controversy which has raged over Family Viewing Time, an official affirmation by the National Association of Broadcasters, FCC, and the networks that television does have impact.

Chapter III
The Family Hour: Sense or Censorship?

From its inception as a national medium in the early fifties television was considered an influence with which to reckon. By 1951 there were reported to be TV sets in 51 percent of New York City homes, and nationally 28 percent of the homes had instruments. The number of sets in use that year numbered 11,748,000. That figure alone indicates that the available audience had become economically attractive. Radio, meanwhile, was suffering a serious decline. Recognizing the new direction, Jack Gould of the *New York Times* authored a provocative series concerning the effects of TV on American life. In the same year, TV producers put together an ethics code for the infant industry. In July of 1951 the NAACP took the question of ethics into their own hands when, sufficiently concerned over TV impact, they protested the image of blacks portrayed by the new series *Amos 'n Andy*. The program experienced a very brief life before expiring. Finally, 1951 was the first year of the transcontinental cable that carried *Dragnet*, *The Millionaire*, and *Gary Moore* from coast to coast.

By 1952 new programs included *Gangbusters*, *I Married Joan*, *Life with Luigi*, *Meet Millie*, *My Friend Irma*, *My Little Margie*, and *Our Miss Brooks*. Working within the established stereotypes, women had a good share of starring roles. The number of TV sets nationally jumped to 15.7 million.

Already perceived as a political force, by 1952 the content of TV drama began to draw fire from official sources for possible subversion. Anticommunism extended a chilling breeze into the artistic community. Vicious attacks leveled by *Red Channels*, a "Report of Communist Influence in Radio and Television," led to suspicion of many actors and writers, even Lucille Ball. Senator Joseph McCarthy became a symbol around which many rallied to attack the TV industry for "un-Americanism." In the heat of the controversy Philip Loeb was dropped from the cast of *The Goldbergs* after his name was listed in *Red Channels*. Within a year Julius and Ethel Rosenberg would be dead, victims of hysteria which gripped the nation. TV was moving in on the family at a time of terror and censorship. Ironically, it was largely through television that the nation was mesmerized by the fear tactics of McCarthy who utilized the medium with great skill to enhance his political career. From early days TV provided instant fame for obscure but ambitious men.

The demise of McCarthy in 1955, also largely due to TV, took some pressure off the networks, but they seem to have continued to exist in fear! It was really in the teeth of these conditions and the attacks upon creative freedom that the so-called golden age of television flowered with *Studio One, U.S. Steel Hour, Playhouse 90, Omnibus,* and *Kraft Theatre.* But it seems generally agreed by intelligent observers that the McCarthy era left permanent scars on the network psyche. Live drama began to be affected by advertisers who "often felt uneasy about political implications." Erik Barnouw, in *Tube of Plenty,* goes on to indicate that "in 1954, and increasingly in 1955, sponsors and their agencies began to demand drastic revisions and to take control of script problems. . . . During 1954-55 anthology writers and directors found sponsors and their agencies increasingly intent on interfering with script matters, dictating changes, vetoing plot details. The series began a rapid decline." [1]

The outrages McCarthy encouraged did not conclude

with his disgrace. The House Committee on Un-American Activities ground on into the late fifties with its attacks upon the entertainment community. Typical of sentiments in that period are the words of Committee Chairman John S. Wood:

> If, by any action of this Committee, we could be instrumental in eliminating from the field of public entertainment the views of people, particularly the youth, who decline to answer a question as to whether they are members of the Communist Party, it would make me extremely happy.[2]

By 1960 several factors had combined to create what approximated a television monolith. The advertising profits were skyrocketing. By 1964 CBS had net profits after taxes of $47.6 million.[3] The number of sets had increased to the point that one could justly talk of a national medium. More and more programs were being designed for mass audience appeal and the result was the expulsion of television drama like *Playhouse 90* to be replaced by *The Real McCoys*. Meanwhile film was eliminating live TV drama and comedy, resulting in the transfer of the balance of creative television talent to the West Coast. Memories in networks were long, and although by 1963 the political climate was markedly different from what it had been only a decade before, caution prevailed in executive suites. In a frank discussion of his years in television Delbert Mann confirmed this chronology. He began in television in 1949, directing Paddy Chayefsky's *Marty* in 1953, and continued until 1959 when he left the medium. He worked in the early sixties on feature films and returned to TV in 1967—in specials. He suggested that the specials, prominent in that period, represented more a network tip of the hat to quality than a trend to better drama.

It had been laughter through situation comedies which

aided in the death blow to quality drama in the late fifties. By 1965 a maturing comedic mentality was raising issues for public consumption in the dialogues of *The Smothers Brothers Show* (CBS) and *Laugh-In* (NBC). Through the former, humor began to attack previously untouched subjects in politics and religion, and the latter injected a greater degree of freedom with reference to sex. Possibly the political arena, torn by Vietnam, assassination, and scandal, was unable to provide a platform for counterattack against new freedoms, resulting in a relaxation of controls. The networks seem to have felt somewhat less pressure. Comedy continued to grow as did the number of studies of violence. But so also did police and detective shows, rising to an all-time high of twenty-four by 1976.[4]

An abrupt challenge to network timidity came in 1971 when Norman Lear took a British idea and successfully sold it to CBS as *All in the Family.* ABC had rejected the same pilot some years before, but with the agreement by CBS to air the Bunkers, traditional aversion to controversy which had characterized most series entertainment programs was cracked wide as well as the "viewers' presumed preference for blandness."[5] The slaphappy era of television with its mindless comedic style was at an end. Lear's success was even more remarkable considering the fate of The *Smothers Brothers Show,* which was removed from the air by CBS in the 1969-70 season. However, *Laugh-In* did continue on NBC and *Mary Tyler Moore* with its new brand of comedy was aired by CBS a year prior to Lear. But with Lear, many observers believe the "floodgates" were opened. Reality coupled with comedy inundated the American family room through a flood of realism in language and ideas. And the Nielsen ratings demonstrated that the public liked it. The proliferation of Lear comedies—*Maude, Good Times, The Jeffersons, One Day At a Time, Mary Hartman, Mary*

Hartman, All's Fair, Sanford and Son—attest to popular encouragement. Complementing this tide were other offerings from MTM and the remarkably distinguished *M.A.S.H.* By 1973 there had developed a confluence of Lear, MTM, *M.A.S.H.*, and the cops. Rumblings were being heard about inappropriate materials for children, originating with parents.

The 1972 Surgeon General's report on violence and television rekindled the debate even as the networks were seemingly conspiring to create the notion that all roads lead to cops and robbers. By the fall of 1975 there were twenty-two detective and police series out of seventy prime-time programs, a 31 percent share. Watergate and its aftermath may be fingered as a contributing cause of this continued climb. Nixon, who had spoken glibly of the Puritan ethic, and who had used the religion game to "con" constitutents and had sought to manage TV news, may have, in his departure from office, touched off an unfocused public desire for more attention to traditional values. This is most difficult to assess, not alone because of the ambiguous nature of the term "traditional values." But it is true that Gerald Ford restored a modicum of calm and docility to the political scene. This combined with his "sincerity" may have given rise to the reemerging of government as a potential controller of ideas, and consequently, national taste. Rising crime rates could have provided a second stimulus for some voters to look to Washington for a form of TV control.

In any case, by 1974 pressures began to mount from various publics concerning "sex and violence" on the networks. Primary targets for such pressure were the Federal Communications Commission (FCC) and the Congress. At the same time, the three networks seemed concerned to maintain their superior position in television over against cable TV, a potential challenger for the same market. Their favored status was largely dependent upon a friendly and sympathetic FCC bureaucracy. Growing numbers of political personalities found instant acceptance when they made critical remarks about prime-time television and its impact upon the nation's youth.

According to the records of the Federal Communications Commission, on November 22, 1974, the executives of the three commercial networks agreed to a "family hour" for prime-time TV. On January 10, 1975, the FCC chairman, Richard Wiley, network representatives, and the National Association of Broadcasters (NAB) met and announced agreement on a "voluntary" family hour. On February 4, 1975, the NAB amended its code to provide for family viewing between seven and nine each evening, to go into effect September, 1975. While no definition of the hour was forthcoming, it was generally agreed that the three networks would police the period to assure programs suitable for the entire family, including children under twelve.

In spite of numerous disclaimers, this writer has reason to believe, based upon informed sources, that Family Viewing Time was a trade-off by the networks who were under severe pressure from the FCC. In exchange, future considerations from the FCC were understood. Some Congressmen have expressed this suspicion, as is witnessed by the letter of November 20, 1975, to Mr. Wiley from members of the House Subcommittee on Communications which reads in part, "members of the Subcommittee are interested in finding out whether the concept of family viewing is essentially an attempt at self-regulation by the industry, or whether it was established primarily in response to 'informal' regulation by the Commission." [7]

At least one observer close to the FCC is strongly of the opinion that the Commission is a "kept" group of intellectual lightweights easily manipulated by the broadcasting interests. Efforts by this writer to confront such questions with Chairman Wiley proved fruitless when the chairman found it necessary to cancel an appointment and offered no effort to establish an alternative date.

One former FCC employee insists that when important issues arise for Commission consideration most of the commissioners do not read the pertinent materials prepared by staff, necessitating the leaking of the data to trade papers which then condense the report for easy reading by commissioners. Of course the trade papers are controlled by broadcast interests.

Regardless of who coined the phrase "family viewing," the evidence is strong in support of the charge that producers, directors, writers, and actors were never consulted.[8] Family Viewing Time (FVT) was thrust upon the American public without careful definition and with dangerous implications for the medium. What were the charges that led to this high-level decision?

While there are many legitimate studies on TV violence and well-researched comments of intelligent critics, none of which can be dismissed easily, such serious and knowledgeable efforts appear to have been only a background against which more emotional reactions moved. In the fall of 1975, *U.S. News and World Report*, in an article entitled "What's Happening to American Morality?" stated without a single supporting document that "what children in the 98 per cent of American households owning television sets see is wholesale assaults on traditional values: extensive drug and alcohol use and abuse, violence, sex, greed and gambling."[9] Having spent three years in intensive viewing of evening TV fare, I find these assertions untrue.

In the first place, the presentation of drugs, violence, and sex is always within the context of traditional law-and-order themes. In fact, family solidarity and traditional values are consistently reinforced as will be demonstrated in the following chapters. Second, no other available communications medium—art, music, radio, theater, records, books, film, newspapers—is as constantly devoted to tradition-conserving themes. The claim that there is too much violence on TV must be separated from the undocumented contention that what one sees on television is a diet of assaults on values.

A specific line of attack has come from certain church or religious leaders. The president of Morality in Media was quoted recently as saying, "If we watch television we find that immorality is the rule, not the exception." [10] Unfortunately, morality being undefined, the same could be said of anything to which a person took exception. Each individual has his or her private definition of morality. As phrased, the charge then appears either ignorant or malicious. Other attacks have been equally obscure and imprecise. One church commission of a major denomination pointed to the "serious problem of immoral television programming," while an educational administrator grandly blamed TV for increased rape and robbery, calling the networks "the enemy" of the church in contemporary society. [11] He based that charge on a single *Today* show interview with Milton Berle. Such ungrounded vilification of an entire industry is becoming more common and may be regarded as a genuine threat to creative freedom in the future. Already congressional nerves and FCC complicity seem to have created, without thought, Family Viewing Time. And in a rush to judgment, many observers, including Senator John Pastore, have looked upon FVT and found it to be good.

Is that conclusion valid? Did the American public require such an hour? Respecting sex and violence, what type of TV programming has received most popular

45

support in the past twelve months? In an effort to answer these and related queries, each of the top twenty-four shows in the Nielsen cumulative ratings for December 21, 1975, was subjected to a brief analysis. What follows is the result of that research.[12]

1. *All in the Family*—a series that has exposed some roots of bigotry while exercising itself on behalf of family solidarity and traditional values as they are challenged by an ever-increasing complexity. Sex is treated with respect, if directly.

2. *Maude*—a show centered around highly opinionated believer in equal justice that has treated with loving care alcoholism, abortion, and depression.

3. *Phyllis*—a brightly polished comedy that pits a mother-daughter relationship against real-life issues within the context of protective family stability.

4. *Sanford and Son*—a delightful vaudeville excursion with no redeeming social value except to make one laugh.

5. *Rhoda*—a real slice of comedic art. Where is the immorality, the sex , the violence? The dialogue if one be honest, is common to the vast majority of Americans.

6. *One Day at a Time*—a new Lear entry seeking to extract the humorous out of a difficult period of divorce adjustment. For anyone with breathing teen-agers the language and idea content are on the mild side of reality.

7. *Six Million Dollar Man*—pure hocum with too much violence gratuitously injected with no identifiable purpose except to suggest that technology is superior to humanity. It appears during FVT.

8. *The Waltons*—needs no comment in this context.

9. *Kojak*—a slick, sometimes overly violent slice of New York police life which is highly mythologized. Kojak is extremely moralistic and he cares. Ethnic issues are dealt with in sensitive fashion. Criminal violence is always punished, there is almost no sex, and the language

is far less profane than that of west end Richmond.

10. *Good Times*—a remarkably successful team who caricature ghetto life in the context of family loyalty and the clash of generations. Morally condemnatory of drug abuse, race bigotry, and societal injustice.

11. *Chico and the Man*—comedy with a touch of the street. Seldom raunchy, never violent, almost never extreme on sex. Again a generation conflict and friendship are highlighted.

12. *The Mary Tyler Moore Show*—better than most sermons heard the next morning.

13. *Starsky and Hutch*—a Spelling and Goldberg romp with no less violence than others of its genre. It often proves offensive due to its sympathetic treatment of the little criminal and constant overplaying of violence in police work.

14. *Little House on the Prairie*—the western *Waltons*.

15. *Streets of San Francisco*—a neatly done police show which exalts moderate to conservative attitudes toward law and the state and justice with generally excellent character study. Much superior to other Quinn Martin offerings. Violence is at a minimum.

16. *Medical Center*—a highly moralistic, pro-life drama, bordering at times on melodrama. Almost no violence. Sex usually related to medical diagnosis.

17. *ABC Sunday Night Movie*—uneven, difficult to comment.

18. *Bob Newhart Show*—a comedy with no violence, little sex, and no offensive language, just fun.

19. *The Jeffersons*—a Lear production that recently has developed the humanity of its hero sufficiently to justify the comedy. Moralistic, protective family with a grown son who lives with and respects his parents. No violence.

20. *The Carol Burnett Show*—an uneven but generally

well-orchestrated comedy variety. On occasion a little heavy on the sex, but its time at 10:00 P.M. (EST) may justify some of this. Sometimes the sexual allusions are gratuitous. No violence. Uneven social comment. The show used to make light of the elderly in a rather vulgar way. This has been eliminated.

21. *Happy Days*—an absolutely delightful reincarnation of *Leave It to Beaver*, which has provided America's youth with a new hero—Fonzie. No violence. Good dialogue and tasteful language.

22. *M*A*S*H*—the class of the competition. No overt violence, only the results of war. Sexual connotations may prove too heavy for some, but it hardly qualifies as immoral.

23. *NFL Football*—the games are violent, sometimes well played. The announcers could qualify as the most obnoxious thing on TV.

24. *Police Woman*—the most vulnerable to the charges of gratuitous sex and violence. While better in its current year, the show still lacks direction and purpose.

In sum, are these the twenty-four shows that we are told combine to corrupt our children, teach them drug abuse, sexual license, violence and rape, robbery and murder? Now really! When one considers the violent and sick events of our world in the recent past, the offerings on TV appear almost escapist.

Lurking behind the FVT decision of the NAB and the networks is the possibility of its further extension. In any event, as it now exists the arbitrary 9:00 P.M. hour hardly proves beneficial since most children remain awake long after that hour, and the suggestion that parents turn off the set after 9:00 is unrealistic and idle moralizing for most parents in an urban setting. The public is caught in a three-way squeeze with the moralizers who want censorship, the creators who want none, and the networks who want to make money.

TV Guide, in what was described as an effort to uncover America's true feelings on family viewing, commissioned a study of attitudes toward Family Viewing Time. The results of the survey were published in the December 6-12, 1975, issue under the title "Does America Want Family Viewing Time? The Answer: a Resounding 'Yes.'" It was claimed that 82 percent of the public favored Family Viewing Time. In fact, a reading of the article revealed that only 30 percent of those interviewed knew "the general fact that 'family viewing time' is a period set aside—at *some* time during the day—for programs appropriate for all members of the family, including young children." Faced with these statistics as "established" (it is not clear whether these results were tabulated before other questions were posed), the respondents were provided with a definition of family hour and 82 percent then favored such a rule. Those who conducted the survey apparently made no effort to determine the reaction to FVT in light of charges that it was coercive and a form of censorship.

A second poll in *TV Guide* of June 5, 1976, asked whether FVT had passed the test. The findings, labeled "startling," confirmed the results of the previous fall. Still 50 percent of the respondents knew nothing about FVT, and only 35 percent were at all familiar with the idea. While a whopping 72 percent of viewers feel there is too much violence on TV, 58 percent find too much emphasis upon sex. These statistics do not seem to be reflected in Nielsen ratings over the past several years.

One might inquire at this juncture about the so-called public outrage at sex and violence on TV. If indeed, such were the real situation among American viewers, how does one explain their almost total ignorance of the

49

supposed solution? None of this would really matter if the survey were not in the process of becoming a public weapon in support of FVT. It is important that TV, any more than other segments of our corporate life, not be controlled on the basis of privately commissioned polls, exact or inexact.

Pursuing the first *TV Guide* poll further, psychologist Dr. Lee Christie, specializing in statistical analysis, has reached some provocative conclusions. Among them: (1) only 7 percent were well informed on FVT; (2) "being more aware of FVT goes with being less favorable to it"; (3) there was no opportunity to be "undecided"; (4) those most likely to object to sex on TV "tend to be old women in households without children"; and (5) 69 percent of those questioned oppose stricter controls on the content of television programs.[14] Editorializing on the poll by the magazine raises interesting questions on this "rush to judgment."

A helpful analysis of FVT for 1975-76 appeared in an unpublished master's thesis by Gurney Wingate Grant at the University of North Carolina. It is entitled "The Family Viewing Concept: A Content Analysis." Grant concludes that "violence was found to occur in the family hour with almost the same frequency as in the post-family hour," but the violence was less painful, not as often fatal, involved fewer lethal weapons, and was based on "more acceptable motives." In contrast, "there is little evidence to indicate that the treatment of 'adult content' during the early hour was 'toned down.'" Respecting the networks, Grant notes, "in terms of the quantity and handling of 'adult content' and the quantity of violence, practice appears to be at variance with principle." Caution is needed here since Grant did employ certain techniques of George Gerbner's (see p. 177), and he may not have overcome all the difficulties in discriminating among

violent acts on the basis of plot content and types of
violence.

It is probably indisputable that the long debate and
extensive research on violence has affected the various
components which established FVT. And it is heartening
to know that intelligent research is not going unnoticed.
Nevertheless, the researchers did not propose solutions
and one wonders about those being offered by self-
appointed moralists. There are, I believe, too many
different publics for the networks to assume a role in
censorship ostensibly to protect children. Nine o'clock is,
for many children, the beginning of viewing after
completion of school assignments. Further, as more and
more children have their own sets, it becomes idle to
presume any conclusions about family viewing without
extensive research. In fact, television may be in the
process of fragmenting families as sets decline in price
below sixty dollars. Today, thanks to transistors and ear
plugs, radios are tiny private companions. Likewise,
technology is making TV an individual or generational
affair. How far down into childhood this phenomenon
will finally reach is only open to speculation. But it has
begun and needs seriously to be considered for the future.

No matter how ill-designed the family hour may be
presently, the suggestion of such an hour or hours raises
some highly significant issues for a free society. As it is
practiced critics have contended it has numerous flaws
among which are: (1) Children remain up long after 9:00
P.M.; (2) criteria for judging suitability for FVT are ill
defined and obscure, if they exist at all; (3) it provides a
subterfuge for greater violence and license after 9:00 P.M.;
(4) it is a politically inspired trade-off between the FCC
and the networks, tending to make it corrupt from the
beginning. To overcome these serious complaints a
reasonable action would be to extend the FVT to 11:00 P.M.

and draw up harder guidelines. Since the potential already exists for such regulations within the present power of the networks over the creative community, it would be relatively easy to require a formal public commitment to police prime time. Violations of good faith might be identified by the FCC. In short, in order to go beyond the informal controls that have been exercised for years by the program practices departments of the three networks, censorship would be the logical next step. The bumbling attempt of 1975-76 to establish it without admitting it has caused, quite naturally, a vigorous reaction from the creative community in California. Its members envision a return to 1953 with its subtle pressures to conform based upon some national hysteria.

If rules were made, who would make them? What morality would prevail? Which pressure groups would receive official sanction? Would program content be governed by Mormons, Southern Baptists, the NAACP, Gay Liberation, Americans for Democratic Action, Ralph Nader, Catholics, the National Rifle Association, Methodists, Democrats, Republicans? The FVT is similar to all efforts at imposed morality in that it risks freedom in the name of righteousness, and the price is high. The networks had best be careful. While they would quickly reject efforts at censorship by the FCC or Congress upon their activities, they seem reasonably content to become submissive to public censorship when dealing with those whom they employ to write, act, direct, and produce. The most satisfactory alternative is self-imposed regulations in a free and open market. The present monopoly, which has been jealously guarded by networks and government, affords limited freedom to the viewer who for that very reason, is presumed to need protection from excessive forays into sex and violence by the monopoly. New networks, additional VHF channels (drop-ins), and cable TV offer the viewing public the best hope for relaxation of channel control economically and ideologically.

FVT is a monopolistic effort to find economic security through public relations. If it is to work effectively and not be a charade, it must finally apply until 11:00 P.M. Once the public becomes aware of the facts there may be a growing demand for exactly that. Delbert Mann seems very close to the truth when he suggests that the creators know the impact of television and should watch what they say to the audience, but the worst sin of all, he believes, is a "censorship-allowing society." He urges that creators be given freedom to offend, to fall on their faces, and to misinform. In allowing this dimension of freedom, television would operate under print media rules, stemming from the First Amendment to the Constitution. As long as a monopoly exists such freedom will not guarantee an equal freedom for viewers. Creator and viewer freedom will come only when a free market opens to a larger array of talent and ideas. The present either/or choice could be expanded, and the "or" would no longer be to turn off the set. As it stands, FVT is at best a stumbling effort to respond to grass roots pressure. At worst, it is a program to muzzle or stifle creative diversity that might intimidate cautious business interests.

From his vantage point, Norman Lear remarked in a recent interview that he is personally concerned that winds of political pressure have determined the action of the networks. He feels "that those winds are winds that care not the least about sex and violence per se, which is the all-purpose club that they level at everything. It's ideas, the expression of ideas. Under the guise of getting at the sex and violence, my concern is that there are people in places who don't want the right of privacy discussed in comedy, who don't want the economic policies chided, who don't want the specter of one man's job insecurity viewed by sixty million others who are suffering the same way. It's that kind of thing under the guise of sex and violence they are going after. That's just simply ideas, asking the public to think while its being entertained."

Demonstrating the same concerns, Alan Alda put it succinctly: "But casual violence on television is awful. I hate to see it. I hate even more to see it censored." Alda commented that he was having trouble with words. *M.A.S.H.*, then scheduled for FVT, was forbidden to use the word "virgin." Foolish, Alda suggested, because it ruled out the possibility of initiating dialogue between parents and children over the meaning of words, and consequently ideas. One might assume that children must wait until "'round yon" Christmas for such a word. And that comment leads to an observation concerning words and morality.

The generation that controls the TV programming has grown up afraid of words. Words used to be a means of intelligent exchange among people. Language was a tool, a means of understanding. Currently, we as a nation have become obsessed with word propriety. Words have become ends. Particular words have come to be identified as "offensive," ignoring attitude and context altogether. By the same token, children who have learned to employ with skill, the "right" words are considered polite and well mannered, whether in fact they are or not. Truth is prized far less than appropriate, "polite" conversation. Words often come to dominate political bureaucracy and business advertising as vehicles of deceit. Word meaning disappears.

For TV executives words now seem to define taste. On their scale *Sonny and Cher* is in better taste than *Maude*. While *Sonny and Cher* displays vulgar contempt for intelligence and the beauty of sex, all in FVT, *Maude* exudes regard for persons and feelings. But Maude's words offend while inuendo retains its vogue as humor. Most citizens can distinguish between vulgarity and realism. Gratuitous sexual allusions or humor at the expense of fragile human relations are generally in poor taste no matter what words are omitted. The bankruptcy of using words as criteria for ethics is nowhere more clearly demonstrated than in the career of Richard Nixon, and in particular in his attack upon Harry Truman's language in 1952. Clergy often use the language of Zion to gloss over genuine theological differences. As a people we need to loosen our puritanical sensitivities that discourage free expression and ignore cultural variety.

One of the most frequently heard justifications for FVT is that it will eliminate violence from the child's vision. The outcry about violence has been so persistent that one might assume the only available fare in prime time is police and killing. We have examined the twenty-four most popular shows and dispelled one side of that myth. But perhaps, one might say, the preponderance of shows are such as to establish a "gore curtain" to be raised at nine o'clock. Without any effort to consider the quality of the schedule detailed below, it was possible in February of 1976, by merely changing from one commercial channel to another, to watch TV seven nights a week, eight until eleven o'clock, without pause, and success-fully to limit exposure to two police and detective shows (*Streets of San Francisco* and *Barnaby Jones*). Such a schedule would include seventeen of the top twenty-five shows for the season. Even a moderate use of PBS and the fair number of specials could eliminate violence from the viewing experience of the most avid addict of TV. This is no defense of networks obsessed with police shows and the saleable nature of violence. But it does suggest that critics are possibly aiming without ammunition by asserting that television is an unremitting, unrestrained assault on "traditional values."

February, 1976

Suggested nonviolent TV week

for commercial networks

Saturday	*Emergency!* (NBC), *The Mary Tyler Moore Show* (CBS), *The Bob Newhart Show* (CBS), *The Carol Burnett Show* (CBS)
Sunday	*World of Disney* (NBC), *The Sonny & Cher Show* (CBS), NBC or ABC Sunday Night Movie
Monday	*Rhoda* (CBS), *Phyllis* (CBS), *All in the Family* (CBS), *Maude* (CBS), *Medical Center* (CBS)
Tuesday	*Happy Days* (ABC), *Laverne & Shirley* (ABC), *M*A*S*H* (CBS), *One Day at a Time* (CBS), *Marcus Welby, M.D.* (ABC)
Wednesday	*Little House on the Prairie* (NBC), *Chico and the Man* (NBC), *The Dumplings* (NBC), *Petrocelli* (NBC)
Thursday	*The Waltons* (CBS), *Streets of San Francisco* (ABC), *Barnaby Jones* (CBS)
Friday	*Sanford and Son* (NBC), *The Practice* (NBC), CBS or ABC Friday Night Movie

It should be noted that this schedule does not include such shows as *Swiss Family Robinson*, *Good Times*, *Grady*, *Donny and Marie*, *The Jeffersons*, and *Doc*. Again, without regard to quality, violence and excessive sex can be avoided almost completely. To be fair, one could also create a violent schedule that would include among others *Almost Anything Goes*, *S.W.A.T.*, *Six Million*

Dollar Man, Kojak, Bronk, On the Rocks, Movin' On, The Rookies, Bionic Woman, Baretta, Blue Knight, Hawaii Five-O, Harry O, and *Rockford Files.* But censorship will not answer the problem. It is the networks' sheep-like penchant for violence and macho images that poses the difficulty. There are at least ten of these shows which should be an embarrassment to the networks. Interestingly enough the often maligned Nielsen ratings may be telling the networks exactly the same thing. Police and detective shows are not doing well, there being only five in the top twenty-five shows in February of 1976. However, using Nielsen can become a dangerous habit because it substitutes quantity for quality, and mass appeal is the single criterion. It is perhaps the best of all times to question the validity of the Nielsens while they support reasonableness. The National Citizens' Committee for Broadcasting is presently engaged in a study to find alternatives to the mass audience, primary tool of the Nielsen ratings. Anyone interested in this nonprofit citizens' group might find their publication *access,* quite informative.

It is significant that in November, 1976 a California Court ruled against FVT because it involved collusion between networks and the FCC and hence violated the First Amendment. ABC and CBS announced plans to appeal. Television as a new technological medium is searching for guidelines. Nothing comparable has fallen upon civilization before and tradition provides few clues. As we seek answers within the context of the free enterprise system, the solution must not be censorship.

Chapter IV
Media Medicine and Morality

A skeptic could reasonably argue that any questions one might pose concerning the social thrust and moral impact of television programming have already been answered by the very dominance of the profit motive in that industry. Certainly, producers must be economically successful in order to survive. However, those who populate the television industry, even the economic royalists, have other interests and goals in addition to the accumulation of wealth and power. A look at how this industry has treated the medical field reveals much about these additional interests and goals.

Historically, television has been cautious in its approach to medical science. Its first venture, called *Medic*, was a well-received and highly realistic examination of surgery. The program sought to document medical case histories and used some actual hospital footage. This series began in 1954 and helped to launch the career of Richard Boone, who, after two years, moved to the lucrative and long-running *Have Gun, Will Travel*. During its brief tenure, *Medic* was praised for its "seriousness and high-mindedness,"[1] even though Jack Gould of the *New York Times* felt it was sometimes marred by sensationalism. However, *Medic* came to an end at least partially because the portrayal of a Cesarean section was condemned, prior to its showing, by Father T. J. Flynn, director of radio and TV for the Roman Catholic Archdiocese of New York. This episode, entitled "The Glorious Red Gallagher," was withdrawn by NBC after protest. General Electric and Proctor and Gamble cancelled their sponsorship of the series, and the Los Angeles County Medical Association withdrew its endorsement. In May of 1956, the *Times* reported that NBC had decided to take *Medic* off the air.[2]

During the 1950s, medicine was a growth industry, a science, a pioneering profession seeking to provide better health and longer life—an extremely serious business. The adversary was disease and/or ignorance. Thus, *Medic* had attempted to convey information on such subjects as alcoholism, civil defense, and birth in a taut and intense manner, without humorous relief. Moreover, because the American public had been conditioned by a tense international political atmosphere and was thinking cold war and brinkmanship, it was prepared to respond in dead earnest even to such trivial television fare as the one-dimensional dramas of the Western genre: *Black Saddle, Wyatt Earp, Wanted: Dead or Alive,* and *Gunsmoke.* No wonder that realistic medical drama was viewed with intensity.

After the demise of *Medic* no immediate medical successor appeared. During the 1960s, however, the Kennedy presidency provided a backdrop for a different perspective on the healing arts. In 1961, *Dr. Kildare* and *Ben Casey* appeared and created two significant cultural heroes. Both shows seemed intent upon capturing the efficiency, alertness, and dedication of youth, through the performances of Richard Chamberlain as Kildare and Vincent Edwards as Casey. Yet, both series also included the tempering influence of elder statesmen in the profession, portrayed by Raymond Massey (Dr. Gillespie) and Sam Jaffe (Dr. Zorba). A central theme seems to have been the "passing of the torch." The reasoned caution and compromise of the older generation were contrasted with the idealism of young surgeons, anxious to try new methods or champion unpopular causes. The setting of a metropolitan hospital for *Dr. Kildare* provided the necessary variety of cases, most requiring surgery, even though the show's producer, David Victor, admits that a surgeon is not really involved daily in the lives of patients.

Since both series survived for five years and became immensely popular and lucrative for advertisers, some comparisons are in order. I have noticed in many hours of viewing over these past several years that ABC seems to be characterized by a certain coarseness of production which contrasts dramatically with the smoothness of NBC. For some curious reason that same comparison applies to the two characters Casey and Kildare.

ABC's Casey was jarring, aggressive, a believer in justice. He consistently expressed anger, at times violently, and he "made waves." His sense of justice transcended the protocol of his profession. He was impatient. He quite often drew a line between the hard, long, underpaid hours of the hospital staff and profitable private practice. And, even as he was teaching doctors, he felt that dedication to principle (an important attribute to the younger generation in 1963) could force one to forego the pleasures of the medical good life.

NBC's Dr. Kildare, in contrast to Ben Casey, was cultured and refined. His education showed. He was respectful of authority. There was just the touch of piety in his demeanor not present in the abrupt righteousness of Casey. Yet, like Casey, Kildare often found just causes more important than surgical techniques, and he was willing to challenge authority for such causes. Casey was an established professional, and as such the writers tended to treat him as static, with no ambition for advancement. Kildare went from first-year intern to chief resident, thus incorporating growth into the plot. When Kildare's progress led producer David Victor to attempt to move him into private practice, NBC was not interested, because the network wished to retain a hospital setting. According to Victor, Marcus Welby "takes up a Dr. Kildare figure in the later years."

The two programs inaugurated the idea of a plot in search of a disease. While *Medic* had focused upon the discipline of medicine, Kildare and Casey dwelt upon its practice. These two doctors, caught up in predictable dramatic structure, were heroic as they combatted the evils of death and ignorance. Since the adversary was inevitably impersonal, the pristine reputation of the medical practitioner was in no danger of becoming tarnished. The doctor/surgeon achieved heroic status for his participation in the human conflicts through his expertise in the profession of medicine. The viewer identified this expertise by the use in the dialogue of technical jargon, effective "medical music," and masked faces but knowing glances.

Little, if any, understanding about illness and health was imparted to the lay public. As far as medical ethics were concerned, these were normally reduced to simplistic issues such as whether to inform a terminal patient of his or her condition. Such issues as medical incompetence, excessive fees, medical school quotas, euthanasia, abortion, birth control, and death with dignity were seldom addressed; and when they were, it was with a gingerly touch. Moreover, these early medical shows did not enjoy the freedom of language that prevails today. A good example is an episode of *Ben Casey* concerning a patient who was impotent. The word "impotent" could not be used, however, and the patient only alluded to his condition by such phrases as "I am not a real man." Had the word "impotent" been allowable in 1963, the script would have diminished by half.

Despite these limitations, medical shows made earlier attempts than other types of shows, such as police and

61

lawyer series, to deal with personal drama. The reason for this was probably that public interest in a weekly bout with disease was limited. The result was that Casey and Kildare became counselors and distributors of justice. They directed attention to humanistic values. Right was defined as standing for a patient against a system that required fighting bureaucratic red tape. Dr. Zorba and Dr. Gillespie were reminders of a gentler age of medicine, but an age no less conspicuous for its human concerns. Since Kildare and Casey were almost devoid of professional errors, their positions became nearly invulnerable.

Reflecting upon his work in Dr. Kildare, producer David Victor says that he believes his television drama "made a definite impact on the image of medicine." Richard Levinson and William Link, the producers and writers who recently had responsibility for *Columbo* and *Ellery Queen*, have a different view. They believe that "popular entertainment does not create social change," but rather reinforces already held attitudes. These two men wrote an early *Kildare* script condemning funeral practices, "but as to whether it helped even one individual avoid exploitation at a time of bereavement we couldn't say. . . . All we can realistically hope for is to touch people aesthetically every now and then, and possibly, over a period of years, add an infinitesimal something to the prevailing climate of opinion."

While a discussion of this matter would consume a chapter in itself, as a professor in the humanities who taught throughout the sixties, I am inclined to agree with Victor's judgment. The quality of idealism and optimism which grasped such a large portion of college students during that period could easily be attracted by the likes of Casey and Kildare. It was not that doctors were seen as holy and incapable of error. Rather, their potential for human service and unselfish utilization of the tools of medicine made the two TV doctors believable, if not typical. Yet, in the bitter years of 1965 through 1968, such idealism melted under the white heat of Vietnam. Both series disappeared after 1966, and three years passed before there was renewal of medical shows.

In some ways, *The Bold Ones* was an effort to recapture the optimism that characterized the beginning of the decade by seeking the elusive "relevance" so prized in that era. This 1969 anthology dealt alternately with a white cop and a black district attorney, three law partners, a crusading senator, and a group of doctors. The doctors' portion of *The Bold Ones* helped revive medicine on television and, in so doing, attempted to engage "substantive issues" objectively, while "not taking a shot at anybody." It also made a greater effort than previous shows to inform the audience about diseases and medical problems being treated. David Hartman, as Dr. Hunter, became a kind of teacher, and he recently commented that the series undertook to "use television to educate and inform while entertaining." On the other hand, while humor had gained slight entry in *Casey* and *Kildare*, it now came into full flower in the exchanges between Drs. Hunter and Stewart, with a quite believable senior medical officer played by E. G. Marshall.

Unfortunately, this ambitious undertaking collapsed in 1972, but not before it set some high standards for its genre. As an example, a 1972 drama, "Quality of Fear," produced by David Levinson, humanely engaged the critical issue of psychological treatment for cancer patients. Only in the privacy of a home setting could such a drama have a substantial impact. No other entertainment forum offers the same ideal conditions leading to significant intimate response.

Marcus Welby, M.D., the second long-running and highly popular medical show produced by David Victor, is a significant departure from previous medical shows in that it examines the work of two family physicians, Welby and Kiley. Before casting, Welby was drawn as a middle-aged man. However, when Robert Young was signed to play the part, the hero evolved into a compassionate senior general practitioner who largely reflects the personality of the star. Welby is a doctor who cares, who visits in homes, who is involved in patients' lives. Victor admits that Welby is "fictionalized, oversentimentalized," but he believes "there *are* some Welbys." Indeed, admittedly for a diminishing portion of Americans, there are still doctors who are concerned with medicine as a healing art rather than as a means to a high standard of living.

Because of the nature of any dramatic series on TV, medical shows often assume a plurality of functions for the hero that may tend to suggest invincibility or even deification. Certainly this was true in the cases of Dr. Casey and Dr. Kildare. And, commenting on a *Welby* episode, student Elizabeth Gay wrote: "The plot is a fantasy, where doctors have time to case the streets for a patient. Superhumans, they not only hold the talisman of medical knowledge but have untold powers of persuasion and marriage counseling. They are superhuman in their devotion to others; they are always right and always know it." There are many who feel this medical glorification has exceeded sound judgment.

In a highly critical article entitled "The Great American Swashbucklers," Peter Schrag asserts that "the deification of medicine goes right on," and "for all their demystification of doctors, the new TV medical shows fail utterly to convey the idea that real health depends on confidence in self-management and the ability to cope."[3] It may be true that TV has failed to convey this idea, but then it is proper to ask whether the idea is valid. It would appear that

Schrag has underestimated the depth of the prevailing, almost sacral character of medicine and healing that goes far beyond a simple and natural respect for the science that has helped to alleviate pain and suffering. The tentative character of life and the role of body health in mind health is intricate and far from obvious. It can neither be reduced to statistics nor overshadowed by affirmations of "peace of mind." Good health is psychologically linked to life itself, and the result is a natural respect for a science that has affected the alleviation of pain and suffering. From ancient times the medicine man has held a place of honor or awe just for this reason, and all the appeal to rationality on earth will not likely eliminate the essential aloneness of a person in a body. Irresponsible and flawed human beings may riddle any profession without thereby bringing discredit upon the underlying validity of the endeavor. No amount of analysis will rob a person of death. And by the same token that death has been a chief instrument in the creation of religious mystery, so also has medicine trod in the same community of fear and despair. Since we do not understand life, are we too ill served to find ourselves reponding to the sacerdotal nature of medicine? In any event, it was not within the power of the TV medical series to create that sentiment and one doubts that it is either possible or necessarily desirable to have these shows attempt to destroy that primal response.

Medical shows are still basically vehicles for dramatic art—some good, some poor. They are part of the popular culture, utilizing the professions as artistic props. And the TV producer, because he lives in the realm of emotion as a script supervisor, usually desires to deal with heroes not anti-heroes. His decision to have heroes determines the unrealistic, oversimplified issues and stereotypical characters often presented in these shows. It is to be hoped that as TV drama matures, other dimensions will find their way more often into new scripts.

The most moralistic doctor has been Joe Gannon, the hero of *Medical Center*, which was first aired in the same year as *Marcus Welby* and, like *Welby*, ran for six seasons. But, whereas Welby is a pragmatic traditionalist, Gannon is "hip." He is a modern matinee idol. Gannon is "cool." Teen-agers, even younger children, made *Medical Center* a decided favorite in the Nielsen ratings.

Dr. Gannon champions causes in the name of openness. His is a "plea for tolerance of any deviation one can come up with"—for example, a friend who desires a transsexual operation. I was told by producer Frank Glicksman that Gannon, "does not pass moral judgment on people." This is a misunderstanding of terms. Gannon is a highly moral man who becomes angry when confronted with injustice. But his moral judments are based on his acceptance of people as individuals, and he resents those who seek to impose their own definitions on others.

Nevertheless, there are times when Gannon reveals that he has strong predetermined attitudes about right and wrong, and, though he is less traditional than his rival Dr. Welby, he is more doctrinaire. In an episode entitled "Aftershock," Gannon remains committed to an absolute "pro-life" perspective and refuses to allow a terminal patient to die, even though the oxygen used by the dying man might deprive at least four healthy persons of the chance to survive. Gannon refuses, in his own words, to "play God." In some instances, Dr. Gannon seems to feel that it is murder not to employ every available means of life support. The notion that God decides upon the time of death is subtly woven into several scripts. Yet the fact that without modern technology and medicines, death would have occurred months or years earlier is apparently ignored. Gannon's perspective is not necessarily right, but proponents of alternate positions, such as "death with dignity," must still take his particular set of values into consideration.

In the 1969 episode "A Life in Waiting," Gannon addresses the issue of abortion and expresses a profound belief in the "value of life." He moralizes heavily upon this theme as it relates to the unborn fetus and indicates that his students would laugh at his ideas. Yet, by the seventies, Gannon could champion the cause of a girl who wanted an abortion even when her parents were opposed to the idea. Obviously, a successful series must recognize cultural shifts and the need for change.[4]

In his capacity as producer of *Medical Center*, Frank Glicksman looked for "subjects that are important, that have something to say." Now, after over 160 episodes of *Medical Center*, he and his associate Don Brinkley feel that they are able to expose more of what is going on in the culture because America's youth are bringing more subjects to the surface. Special interest groups insist on being heard, and interestingly, Brinkley believes that pressure groups have forced the networks to deal with issues they would have previously buried under the rug. As we noted with *Medic*, pressure can operate both ways. However, the security against one point of view becoming dominant is the collaborative nature of the industry itself with its internal checks that tend to exclude excesses.

If the two recent giants of the medical genre, *Marcus Welby, M.D.* and *Medical Center*, have a major common flaw, it may have to do with the neat, elegant, traditional, middle-class settings both present. If patients are from other than white middle- or upper-class environments their presence seems to require explanation. However, because the university setting of *Medical Center* is clearly upper middle-class, the clientele is certainly realistic. The same is true of Marcus Welby's practice. Perhaps Richard

Levinson is right when he says that the "people who make TV only know upper middle-class."

Women in these medical series are often represented in stereotyped ways. A recent content analysis of fifteen select shows found, at least in that limited sample, an overwhelming predominance of white male doctors and young white female nurses.[5] *Marcus Welby,* for example, presents a rather traditional perspective on women. Although Dr. Welby's office is in his home, he has no wife. David Victor justifies this omission by pointing out that there was "no function for a wife in the series." Male dominance is presumed, reinforced by receptionist Consuelo Lopez who carries the freight for the minority ethnic group while also performing the "proper" womanly functions as a protective, emotional, and efficient employee. The past season provided marriage for Dr. Kiley, a giant leap for TV physicians, but it had little practical effect upon the plots.

The male dominance of the *Welby* program is gentle and paternalistic, but nevertheless, it is a clear-cut affirmation of the primary role of men in medicine. This is not to say that *Welby* is unusual in its treatment of women. Certainly, neither *Welby* nor *Medical Center* provide adequate professional models for women and girls who watch these shows. Even on the occasions when women are presented as full-fledged doctors, they have their special place.

In one memorable episode of *Ben Casey,* Maggie, the female doctor, was portrayed as learning her place as a woman through counseling a patient.[6]

Female patient: What can I do to help my husband?
Maggie: Let him make the decisions. Let him decide who your friends are.
Female patient: That will change my whole way of life.
Maggie: Isn't that what getting married means?

> Casey to Maggie concerning a date: What do you want to
> do?
> Maggie: I'm not going to make that mistake. I'll do what you
> want to do.
> Male doctor colleague: Who says doctors don't learn from
> their patients?

And it should also be noted that this treatment of women is not confined to television's medical programs. Women have little more than traditional roles on police and detective series. Angie Dickinson may be the star of *Police Woman*, but she is essentially a weekly setup for male entrapment, a traditional female part. McMillan's wife is largely decorative; Columbo has an invisible but vocal Italian stereotype for a wife; Petrocelli's wife is a secretary. Most recently, the bionic woman has appeared as a "co-equal" to the six million dollar man, but she chooses to spend her time between adventures as a school teacher!

At the same time, it is important to remember that this representation of women is a realistic one that does reflect things as they presently are. At a recent dental board hearing in Virginia (the entire State Board was male), a presentation in support of a controversial dental assistance program, nationally funded by the Department of Health, Education, and Welfare, included a slide presentation from HEW. The slides represented all dentists now and for the future as men, while most of the proposed dental assistants were women. Even HEW, when it is not thinking "women's rights," falls into long-held presumptions. In fact, Marcus Welby is more enlightened on this subject than many actual physicians seem to be. Though he resides in a traditional, picket-fence world, he is a liberated man, accepting the new growth of independence and freedom for all persons.

But does any of this really make any difference? Don't

most people watch TV for entertainment and relaxation? Probably the answer is affirmative. Yet, as we are entertained, our minds do function. The reinforcement of values and principles in long-running shows surely must have impact. On this point, social scientists, network executives, writers, advertisers, producers, and humanists generally agree. Gannon and Welby, Casey and Kildare have reinforced some highly traditional values: honesty, trust, justice, freedom, tolerance, equality, education, family, hard work, discipline. Producer Richard Levinson, who would demur on any claim of permanent influence, does contend that conventional liberal attitudes have dominated television for the past fifteen years. Critic Michael Novak concurs: "We are lucky that the social class responsible for the creative side of television is not a reactionary and frankly illiberal class."[7] TV programs seem to conserve historically recognized, Western ethical value structures within the context of "conventional" liberalism. For the present, given the oligopolistic capitalism in the three networks, and given our diverse political and religious affiliations, this may be a healthy compromise.

Of all the "values" considered by the medical programs, the question of trust may prove the most unsettling as it is portrayed in patient-doctor relationships. Patients are seldom represented as thinking rationally about their diseases. (*The Bold Ones* is an exception.) Instead, patients show irrational fear, misunderstanding, and resentment. No answer is provided to the question of how one may be assured that a particular doctor is worthy of trust. Pennsylvania Insurance Commissioner William Sheppard blamed *Marcus Welby* for causing the public to expect much more of doctors," and he claimed "the series might be one reason for an increase in malpractice suits."[8] Of course, being human, doctors do not measure up to their TV models, and the most recent forays into medical drama have attempted to cope with that matter.

NBC observed the marked success of its two competitors in the medical program field and decided to make two new entries into the 1975 ratings war. By the end of November, both *Medical Story* and *Doctors' Hospital* were casualties of Nielsen. Despite critical acclaim, the former lost its place to less imaginative programming.

In its first showing, NBC's *Medical Story* made a serious attempt to deal with malpractice and incompetence in the profession. In this episode, Dr. Ducker, an intern, struggles to prevent an operation by an established surgeon. He fails, as is illustrated in the following dialogue with the chief surgeon of Ducker's division in the hospital, a respected physician on the executive board.

Ducker: They are operating on Donnelly in the morning. [He explains the risks.]

Chief: What has this to do with me, Ducker?

Ducker: I'm going to ask you to put a call in to the board.

Chief: It's not my case.

Ducker: But you verified my findings. I want you to call the board.

Chief: You want me to call the board or are you ordering me to?

Ducker: I'm sorry sir. I don't know who to go to.

Chief: We can't have doctors interfering in other people's cases. It will cause chaos.

Ducker: I told you the symptoms, I told you what he [the surgeon] was doing. Are you saying you don't want to interfere because it would be bad form?

Chief: How do I know Dr. Nolan isn't right?

Ducker: I see. Yeah! We are all members of the same club. There are certain things that we don't do even if a person's life is at stake.

Chief: I think you better go.

As it turns out, the operation does prove to be a mistake. The patient dies and the hospital board has to admit that Dr. Nolan was wrong and Ducker was right. There follows a closing scene:

> Chief: The board is not going to renew your contract. It would cause too many tensions. . . . We are going to give you letters of recommendations. . . . This is an organization like anything else. Some things have to be sacrificed for larger things.
>
> Ducker: What if I go to the papers . . . the accrediting committee?
>
> Chief: I wouldn't do that. You need your letters of recommendation. You'll find there is a tendency to close ranks within the medical profession. If you haven't learned anything else from this episode you should have learned that.
>
> Ducker: I learned that.
>
> Chief: . . . You can't win.
>
> Ducker: All right, I'm fired, but I'm still going to be a doctor.

This anthology continued to investigate, on a weekly basis, such issues as the meaning of death with dignity, the use of patients as objects of experimentation, abortion, industrial poisoning, malpractice, and sterilization. There were still heroes, but they did not necessarily find success within the system. It was ironic to see Vincent Edwards (playing a new doctor, but with his old Ben Casey posture still unchanged) handcuffed by police and taken into custody for performing an alleged illegal abortion. This episode ends with the surgeon in question saying he will leave the matter in the hands of the court. And, venturing even further into uncharted television territory, this episode portrays a priest as a "heavy." The words of Cleveland Amory seem appropriate: "Imagine a doctor show without a pat or a happy ending. We tell you it's a medical millennium."⁹ Well, not exactly. The program was not popular and *Medical Story* fell to sixtieth place by late October. Despite brave predictions from NBC executives, economics dictated cancellation.

Doctors' Hospital was more traditional than *Medical Story*, but it suffered the same fate. George Peppard as a neurosurgeon reminded us of Ben Casey, but there was an update. Like *Medical Story*, this series gave sympathetic treatment to the role of women in medicine. There were flirtations with serious professional issues. In one particular episode, a woman surgeon is faced with the ultimate questions of life that finally tear at the presumption of medical diety. Then, out of a plethora of philosophizing reminiscent of Ecclesiastes, there emerges an essentially nontheistic humanism: "All there is is life and all that you can do is celebrate it."

The answer to why *Welby* and *Medical Center* survived, while two new competing efforts have failed, is not easily discovered. Familiarity certainly played a part. Competition in the allotted time slots is also an important consideration. However, I am inclined to believe that the TV medical show is historically in a distinct category. At no time since 1950 have more than three medical programs been simultaneously and successfully sustained. Yet the success that the industry has found in spin-offs and copies of other types of shows may have led executives and producers to expect the same principles to apply in the medical shows. I doubt that they do.

It is probable that the public reaches a saturation point in this area very quickly. For one thing, there is a strong viewer identification with the principle doctor characters of medical shows. Many supporters of one series tend to ignore other series. Part of the reason for this phenomenon may be that few of us consistently have more than one or two doctors attending us. Moreover, healing is an art with which we have frequent contact. Hospital visits are as common for most of us as prison and police station visits are rare. This surfeit of medicine in our personal lives may cause us to reject too much medicine on TV.

Also, another important reason for the failure of such series as *Medical Story* may be that the public simply does not wish to have its trust in doctors challenged so directly. Viewers still seem more satisfied with medical shows that present familiar perspectives in health care and that tend to reinforce the already positive image of the doctor in society. The public's medical hero is a model of integrity, good citizenship, professionalism, and human kindness. And, on top of all these virtues, he is a believer in the ethic of hard work.

Medical shows that promote such superdoctors might easily convince one that the field of medicine is almost totally populated with professionals whose only commitment is to service. The economic rewards of the profession are not questioned, and one would scarcely guess that there are vast numbers of citizens living in poverty and discovering that their level of existence does not entitle them to receive the medical services which their TV sets promise them.

However distorted this altogether positive image of medical professionals as a whole may be, it is easy to understand that it is an accurate reflection of society's desires. People still want to believe in their doctors. The vast majority of seriously ill patients still want to believe that "if there is a cure," then their doctor will find the surgeons or other specialists to attack the disease. Because the ultimate concerns of these medical shows—the mysteries of life, sickness, and death—are profound, attitudes about them change slowly, and the history of the genre suggests that successful programs cannot differ greatly from the prevailing attitudes and beliefs of their audience.

Yet a few successful shows have given attention to the critical issues of medical ethics—malpractice, euthanasia, genetics, fee structures, hospital costs. During its brief tenure, *Medical Story* opened many of these issues for viewing and challenged the mythic image of doctors. For instance, *Medical Story* raised the suspicion that one's doctor might not know "the cure" and that, if he did, his personal character could affect the outcome of the case as significantly as the procedure he chose to use. Despite the fact that *Medical Story* met an untimely death, its presence on NBC for almost four months points to a qualitative leap in the treatment of medical drama.

Of course, the medical dramas intend to entertain, and it is within this frame of reference that discussion of impact must occur. But current medical dramas also show every intention of including moral and ethical comment as well—a motive that is certainly not antithetical to good entertainment. Although traditionalism remains a strong element in most medical series, there are messages being delivered. There are also challenges to modern medical practices, and a few more realistic medical models. This continuing struggle over humanistic values portrayed on the tube may have a salutary effect on viewers, and some producers in the television industry believe that there are still ways to develop greater maturity in TV medicine.

That there is a connection between television's medical shows and societal conditions seems clear. However, which has the greater influence on the other is less clear. Are we being conditioned, or are we merely viewing reflections of ourselves and our culture on TV? Probably there is some of both. Yet the public is showing increased interest in the issues of medical science, as the Quinlan euthanasia controversy verifies. And if it is true, as recent disclosures in nationally published inquiries suggest, that 5 percent of practicing physicians are incompetent,[10] then the possibility that doctor shows are causing more malpractice suits may be an encouraging sign. We can be hopeful that greater expectations will produce more responsible doctors. In any case, whether they are a cause or an effect in society, television's medical shows are a unique and significant forum for public consideration of questions which literally are matters of life and death.

Chapter V
Television Drama

HIGH-MINDED VIOLENCE?

In spite of the large number of police and detective shows populating prime-time schedules there is no simple formula by which they can be lumped together. From *Columbo*, the classic "city mouse-country mouse" confrontation, to *Kojak*, a slick, well-produced fantasy, to *Police Story*, a realistic cut of police activities, to *Cannon*, the humorless tracker of evildoers in absurd settings, the spectrum is broad and few generalizations apply. The one common denominator of all these series is violence. Death and murder are mainstays of each. So in a broad sense one might describe them as violent programs. But discrimination must be employed to separate *S.W.A.T.* from *Ellery Queen* or any rational discussion is impossible.

Quite naturally in the present climate almost all producers of such dramas are sensitive when violence is mentioned. And, as expected, violence itself in plot development is viewed differently from show to show. An overview of the problem was offered by Alan Alda whose series, *M.A.S.H.*, is uniquely associated with the consequences of violence.

> There is just as much violence in most of Shakespeare's tragedies as there is in any hour television police story. The difference is the people respond to it with a human response. Very often producers will think that they have reduced the level of violence if they keep it off camera and sweep it under the rug as fast as possible and have people go

on as if nothing had happened. But on the contrary, according to my way of thinking, that's very inhuman and it conditions the audience. It's one of the unspoken assumptions that violence can be tolerated as long as you ignore it and as long as you have no reaction to it. [But that] leads to psychopathic behavior. It leads to an acceptance on the part of the country for the Vietnam War. I think the Vietnam War is the product of dozens and dozens of Western movies where Indians were shot off their horses and people laughed and went on with their love story.

Alda may have struck upon an important distinction respecting impact. The general procedure in research has been to estimate impact by a study of individual behavior responses to TV action. The results have been inconclusive. But what of the corporate effect? Does television drama and comedy, not to mention news, encourage social acceptance of acts and deeds by others that might never present themselves as options of personal choice? Could they precipitate agreement to violent national policy? One measure of this conditioning is to be observed in a recent experiment which I believe relates directly to the revelations about the CIA and the FBI. I reported to a morning class quite seriously that I had just heard on the news that Lyndon Johnson was responsible for the death of President Kennedy. The reaction was startling. My story was believed and, in fact, there was no shock, only questions about how he was found out. Now this does not demonstrate that my students would cook up assassination plots, but it does strongly suggest that official sanction of this type of behavior has become a national way of life. Resignation has become an appropriate response to many who feel hopelessly remote from seats of power.

Literally reams of paper have carried the debate over violence on television since the earliest days of programming. A classic study, *Television and the Child*, appearing in 1958, pointed to the "increased maladjustment and delinquent behaviour" of children and expressed the belief that violence on television would "blunt their [children's] sensitivity to suffering." The book urged alternative approaches to crime and violence programs that would "present themes and characterizations which are morally and socially more worthwhile."[1] As a corollary to its findings it was suggested that "television planners can greatly influence children's taste."

Since 1958 a massive amount of time and energy has been expended on the question of violence. Increasing numbers of social scientists have attempted to isolate groups for intensive study. The names of Tannenbaum, Bandura, Berkowitz, and Feshbach are associated with four different theories of aggression presumed to be caused by TV violence. Their research led, in 1972, to the Surgeon General's report, *Television and Social Behavior*, which concluded there was some correlation between TV violence and aggression.

> The experimental studies bearing on the effects of aggressive television entertainment content on children support certain conclusions. First, violence depicted on television can immediately or shortly thereafter induce mimicking or copying by children. Second, under certain circumstances television violence can instigate an increase in aggressive acts. The accumulated evidence, however, does not warrant the conclusion that televised violence has a uniformly adverse effect nor the conclusion that it has an adverse effect on the majority of children. It cannot even be said that the majority of the children in the various studies we have reviewed showed an increase in aggressive behavior in response to the violent fare to which they were exposed. The evidence does indicate that televised violence may lead to increased aggressive behavior in certain subgroups of

children, who might constitute a small portion or a substantial proportion of the total population of young television viewers. We cannot estimate the size of the fraction, however, since the available evidence does not come from cross-section samples of the entire American population of children.

. . . There is evidence that among young children (ages four to six) those most responsive to television violence are those who are highly aggressive to start with—who are prone to engage in spontaneous aggressive actions against their playmates and, in the case of boys, who display pleasure in viewing violence being inflicted upon others.

. . . The lack of uniformity in the extensive data now at hand is much too impressive to warrant the expectation that better measures of aggression or other methodological refinements will suddenly allow us to see a uniform effect.[2]

The central conclusion, that those children with a propensity to violence are more responsive to TV aggression, is reasonable and substantiated by other independent study.[3] Sociologist Herbert Gans believes "the prime effect of the media is to reinforce already existing behavior and attitudes, rather than to create new ones."[4] He is supported in this view, as we noted previously, by producers William Link and Richard Levinson who believe TV has no real impact toward change, but only reinforces.

Still the studies proliferate. The August, 1975, issue of the *Journal of Communication* devoted itself almost entirely to "TV's Effects on Children and Adolescents." In June of 1975, *TV Guide* was still asking on its cover "Violence! On TV—Does It Affect Our Society?" Actually, the question the magazine posed for "six outstanding men" was not whether violence on TV affects society, but how? In fact, even the social scientists have not arrived at an acceptable common definition of violence. Beyond killing and maiming, what is violence?

Professor George Gerbner of the Annenberg School of Communications of the University of Pennsylvania is quite inclusive in his violence definition and in relation thereto proposes a rather sinister analysis. He has, for several seasons, been preparing a yearly violence profile or index based upon saturation viewing of one week's programs. While identifying a high level of violence, there is imprecision in definition and categorizing.[5] From his findings he has devised a fascinating thesis, recently articulated in *Human Behavior*.

> Our research shows that heavy viewing of television cultivates a sense of risk and danger in real life. Fear invites aggression that provokes still more fear and repression. The pattern of violence on TV may thus bolster a structure of social controls even as it appears to threaten it.
> . . . Television is the universal curriculum of young and old, the common symbolic environment in which we all live. Its true predecessor is not any other medium but religion—the organic pattern of explanatory symbolism that once animated total communities' sense of reality and value, and whose relationship to the state is also governed by the First Amendment.[6]

This thesis combines two major assumptions. In the first place, it is asserted that the "symbolic representation of violence and sex in the mainstream of our culture has become a battleground in the larger struggle for control of that mainstream." In other words, Gerbner believes there is a conspiracy to bring the American population to heel by injecting a fear of violence and an acceptance of it as the means of state solution to problems. Gerbner asks if the business establishment would risk costly social disruption for bigger profits unless some more powerful motive were at work. He admits we must be subjected to this scheme for "a long time" in order for it to accomplish its presumed effect.

In response it could be asked whether assuming such a high degree of sophistication among business interests in this country is realistic. And certainly such interests are neither monolithic nor politically uniform. One need not doubt the fact that some business magnates envision the glory of a *Rollerball* millennium in order to reject as unsatisfactory a conspiracy theory of the magnitude required for the Gerbner thesis. And, in spite of the Gerbner studies, TV violence is not so clearly uniform. Finally, the long history of violent solutions to problems in this nation, the extensive personal stake which many citizens express in gun ownership, belie the theory Gerbner develops. Business has no real evidence that TV drama violence would "risk costly social disruption" and therefore the urge for profit requires no correlative "more powerful motive."

A second intriguing point that Gerbner sets forth concerns the replacement of religion by television. If religion can be defined, such definition must include the notion of ultimate concern. Religion is that to which one gives primary allegiance above all else in life. It could be God, or security, or nation, or ideology, or self. But TV, lacking humanity, history, tradition, symbol, and ritual can hardly be legitimately termed a replacement for religion. It is, of course, not demonstrated by Gerbner that such replacement has occurred. Certainly, television might become a ritual act of a civil religion, a reflection of the consuming appetite of nationalism. But a ritual act is not religion; it is, rather, a symptom of what one holds ultimately significant.

If, in the final analysis, a simpler, less convoluted explanation for the presence of much violence on television is called for, that does not thereby relieve the responsibility for inquiry into the nature of its presentation. How then is violence employed in prime-time TV?

Nothing in this investigation loomed as so mammoth an undertaking as the analysis of the police-detective genre. In over a quarter century of commercial television there has never been as large a number of these shows on the air as at present. Of course, public and private investigators of crime have frequented the airwaves since the forties. Martin Kane, Ellery Queen, Boston Blackie, and Mark Saber were all at work by 1952. And it was in that year Jack Webb brought *Dragnet* to the screen, a show that, in different forms, continued with interruptions until 1974. *Highway Patrol* introduced "ten-four" to our vocabulary and perpetuated the image of Broderick Crawford as the no-nonsense state trooper. However, in the fifties, as new dramas were added old acquaintances departed so that at no time did the number of police-detective series exceed seven in a season. The year 1958 seems to have been pivotal for changing style, for it was then that the networks introduced *77 Sunset Strip, Naked City, Peter Gunn*, and *The Untouchables*, followed a year later by *Hawaiian Eye* and *The Detectives*. These series were primarily humorless affirmations of law and order with little attention to levels of violence. Ethnic slurs concerned critics of *The Untouchables* far more than excessive brutality.

Violence had become cheap with the growing supply of Westerns that began to appear in 1955 and numbered fourteen by 1960. The years of no wars and a retiring grandfather as president provided a backdrop for unrestrained violence on the tube with little apparent effort at social relevance. In 1962 an investigation of TV violence by the U.S. Senate tended to reduce bloodshed, and in 1963 all detective and police series had disappeared. Westerns were on the wane, reduced by half from the peak year of 1960. For the season 1964-65 there were neither new police dramas nor any holdovers. While there is lack of hard evidence, it is interesting to speculate upon the correlation between the assassination of John Kennedy in 1963 and the absence of such dramas.

For 1965-66 there began a new violence recipe, the spy shows, inspired it appears by the FBI and the CIA. *I Spy, Get Smart,* and *Secret Agent* joined *The Man from U.N.C.L.E.*, which had premiered the previous year. By 1964 Westerns had diminished to four and within ten years they completely disappeared. In the fall of 1975 the twenty-two police-detective series had representation in the top twenty Nielsen-rated shows in the same proportion as they had in the total schedule. However, by January, 1976, of the twenty-four shows with ratings of twenty or better in the cumulative averages, only four police shows remained. In the fall of 1976 there were sixteen police-detective shows scheduled for prime time including four new offerings. Some are quick to claim the cycle has run its course. But the persistent appeal of police series has suggested a strong market for the product during varying degrees of social and political upheaval. For the purposes of the present chapter we will examine six police dramas in an attempt to discover underlying similarities that might explain popularity and identify moral presuppositions distinctive to some or all.

Police Story

In 1973 a unique concept in police drama emerged from NBC. Carefully fashioned, this anthology of police work insists "upon pressing for a moral point of view." Producers Liam O'Brien and Stan Kallis consider the show to be an exception from a system against which they constantly struggle. In fact these two highly motivated men feel that they probably are at odds with the networks when they object to "the immorality of a system that forces everything in that system to contribute to that morality." O'Brien senses that network executives continue to demand violence because they believe audiences love it. The Surgeon General's report agrees, noting "the remarkable popularity among the adult population of television drama that includes violence is a social reality that cannot be avoided." [7] Interestingly, even when ratings do not support them, executives continue to order more potentially violent episodes.

By the summer of 1976 O'Brien was producing the show alone. Commenting on the cause of so many "action" shows, he noted, "the networks basically believe they are going to sell beer, toothpaste, and all the other things. . . . They are really not an entertainment medium; they are a money-making medium. They say they think 'action' keeps people awake."

Police Story lacks a sustaining cast because of its nature. The individual dramas allow great concentration upon character development and plot line, unencumbered by the idiosyncratic nature of a star-oriented drama. It is considered by professionals to be genuine and its realism comes from a technique described by O'Brien. Each week several policemen from the California area are interviewed by the production staff of the series. From taped interviews are culled those items most likely to develop into workable plots. The policemen, in selected interviews, are requested to return and continue conversation. The stories begin at the human end of the situation. It seems to require an average of fifteen interviews for every one story line uncovered. Discussing the role of TV in the lives of children, O'Brien was quick to assert that the "happy geography of childhood has been narrowed down," and yet he correctly insisted that we "cannot render the scene antiseptic" by withdrawing the TV set.

Police Story adheres to certain principles in plot

85

development. Although they did the original *S.W.A.T.* episode, the producers refused to expand it to a series because of the quasi-fascist implications. Of twenty-two *Police Story* episodes which I reviewed in depth, four involved some type of murder, five were concerned with theft, two with rape, and four with drugs. The seven remaining, while spreading a crime backdrop, employed an effective technique of concentration upon internal conflicts among police or personal problems stemming from police work. This is a satisfying distribution and supports a contention that in spite of its anthological nature, this series presents a more inclusive picture of police work than do those shows which depend week after week upon a single type of crime, murder. While in most police series murder and felonious crime are regularly linked, FBI statistics inform us that nearly 80 percent of murders in America are crimes of passion resulting from rage, jealousy, arguments over property, and revenge, and these involve families or acquaintances. Little more than 15 percent of national homicides result from a felony.[8] *Police Story* holds these facts in perspective.

In a particularly poignant piece broadcast in the winter of 1975 the plot sought effectively to relay several messages. A married policeman, highly regarded on the force, fell in love with an elementary school teacher, also well respected in her profession. The policeman's estranged wife asked the department to put a stop to her husband's extramarital activities. The internal affairs division used undercover methods, threats, and blackmail against teacher and officer alike on the grounds that their relationship was deleterious to the public image of police work. The pressure worked and the lovers separated. The officer was gunned down while making an arrest because his mind wandered to his personal tragedy. In one hour the episode raised moral questions related to marital fidelity, divorce, intimidation, and personal freedom. The relationship between the two lovers was perceived by the producers as a good; yet the problem was complicated by two young daughters whom the officer loved. Out of this maze of human conflict there arose a pointed claim for personal freedom within the context of love.

Such moral drama flies in the face of old-line moralisms of the Protestant Puritan ethic and the theology of the Roman Catholic Church. Both would find fault with this morality play; yet the effective dealing with human relations raises a critical question. Can the networks be guided by any one established set of moral principles? Challenging to certain traditional values though it was, the story was executed within the confines of its own moral position—love and freedom. Morality here, as often on TV, neither presumes the existence of God or Christian moral theology, and that alters the ancient rules in the game of "ethics." Alternative presumptions about human relations and their motivation sometimes cause churches to cry "immoral." But in our society no single moral code can or should be imposed upon TV producers. Religious communities, rather than seeking to maintain their peculiar ethical stance to the exclusion of options, should, I believe, be in the market of exchange, using persuasion, not muscle or censorship. The ethical monolith no longer survives and the Protestant establishment is at an end. Reason in our multiculture requires of the religious institutions a search for foundations of understanding, perhaps beginning with good taste.

Institutional moral purists must also grapple with the matter of history. "Illicit" love affairs have been a constant fact of public life in America, and any legitimate historical treatment cannot ignore facts. Neither in reflection nor in projection should one moral perspective become a controlling force on the airwaves, anymore than should a single political party.

Another evidence that O'Brien and Kallis try to put in a point of view was exemplified by "Little Boy Lost," a strong statement of parental responsibility to children, drawn again from experience of a Los Angeles policeman. The humaneness of the drama incorporates what O'Brien saw in the real life situation. Moving from the nugget of material which is not in "conflict with our general point of view" the producers shape the plot. They did not create the plot to say something. Rather, the character of the story line which initially attracted them provides the value statements.

On occasion a moral is cast in paradoxical terms. A policeman, well regarded by his peers, had too many shootings on his record for the good reputation of his department. The conflict between career and instinct of a cop finally crushed in upon Officer Billy Humm. The questions arose: What is the role of violence in police work? And how does society solve that problem? In that instance, violence itself was confronted as a moral dilemma and no simple solution was offered. The audience is left to cogitate the problem.

Kallis and O'Brien are vigorous, alert, and opinionated men who feel strongly that they have something to say. Network oligarchy seems to them a violation of antitrust laws. As Kallis observed, "If we offend one network we are out of one third of the market." Battling for their position they have provided intelligent, thoughtful drama far from Richard Diamond, Peter Gunn, and Eliot Ness. Though popular with police across the nation, the series, until recently, has been marginal in the Nielsen ratings. For the morally sensitive viewer an Emmy award in May, 1976, is an encouraging omen of greater longevity for the series.

The Streets of San Francisco

Another police show that employs dramatic style that captures something other than the violence of crime is *The Streets of San Francisco*. This popular product of the slick Quinn Martin enterprise is more than a cut above his other recent offerings, *Barnaby Jones* and *Cannon*. A clear law-and-order theme emerges in the context of patriotism and traditional values. But it is done with a reasonable respect for alternative ideas and concepts. The contrasting attitudes toward law and law enforcement at large in the nation are nicely balanced.

An episode aired in 1975 is a good example of several efforts by this series to approach character analysis. Pat Hingle played the part of a salesman, a failure to everyone but his wife. The way in which he was entrapped by his own desperate needs until he narrowly escaped being the victim of a murderer gave far more attention to the all-too-common Willy Loman syndrome than to either police work or crime. It was an absorbing hour.

This series does have some recurring assumptions that invite evaluation. It seems, for one thing, that the producers focus upon a generally optimistic view of human nature which often results too easily in a dichotomy between criminals and victims. The show tends to a simplistic caricature of younger criminals, and the social roots of crime are seldom explored. On occasion, the series attempts a bit of amateur psychology, but even so the very injection of that dimension into the plot is a healthy exception to most police drama.

The younger partner, a college graduate, has been well acted by Michael Douglas, and though by implication wisdom comes with age (Karl Malden) and techniques with education, the younger detective is not an offensive stereotype like the lawyer–truck driver of *Movin' On*.

Steve Keller is an intelligent, socially concerned cop, having chosen the career over law for philosophical reasons. He offers, therefore, a very positive image of professional law enforcement.

The scripts are sometimes uneven and, seeking to convey a message, say it poorly. In a recent hour, a demented teacher incarcerated four academic misfits and sought to force learning on them. The old man died, but in an emotional conclusion a black youth went back to high school because the old fellow cared. The complexity of circumstances that caused the boy to be a dropout were never considered. There was a suggestion that harsh corporal punishment might lead to learning among those who are disadvantaged or delinquent. Hidden within the plot was the idea that learning should touch the motive and the life of the learner. Good! But that theme was heavily distorted by the nature of the plot.

The police in this drama are always respectful of the law, and the conclusions are upbeat with successful completion of a task. Violence is seldom used except within the rules governing the police, and explicit killing scenes are avoided. It is a serious look at police work with certain underlying conservative assumptions about crime and the society. The mid-sixties politicized the police, the result probably of unwise bureaucracy and poor administrative leadership. Unfortunately, since that time liberals have been unfairly categorized as haters of the cops and conservatives as police supporters. *Black Bird*, a recent cinema offering, caricatured this mentality when Sam Spade, the hero, said to a hired thug who had spoken respectfully of the police, "I never heard of a conservative criminal." *Police Story* and *The Streets of San Francisco* provide a good balance to avert the danger of continued national polarization of opinion concerning the security arm of the society.

The two other offerings from QM, *Barnaby Jones* and *Cannon*, are, in contrast, almost insulting to the viewer. The scripts are uniformly poor with ridiculous dialogue and situations. If one rejects the possibility of an updated attempt at "camp" à la *Batman*, Cannon seems to have been created to provide an excuse for gunplay. He is so exceptionally serious that attentive twelve-year-olds guffaw at his lines. Dialogue is intense, undramatic, and unreal. If there are moral assumptions adrift in this disaster they escape notice. The show is the moral! Guns answer problems and violence is a prop for plot. At best it was, until cancelled, a sleepy diversion for viewers seeking escape.

Buddy Ebsen, now Barnaby Jones, looks every bit afraid that he might relapse into the role of Jed Clampett as he sorts out pieces of evidence coupled with ridiculously simple conversation. At least Barnaby has some humor about him, albeit seldom. Both series create heroes who constantly moralize about crime—Cannon with sermons, Jones with knowing sighs and stares. The plots do not support the preachments.

Columbo

William Link and Richard Levinson, who produce this portion of the NBC *Sunday Night Mystery Movie,* admit that the hero is not realistic. He is solving a puzzle in a classic detective story style. The settings allow for the continuing theme of "money brought low by the poor." But Levinson reminded me that "you can't take Columbo seriously." And of course he is right. It is essentially a quiet, enjoyable, well-produced "who dunnit." If the moral ambiguity of making murder a prop for fun is put aside, one can be well entertained. There may, however, be a moral in the play itself. The presentment of monied people constantly involved in intrigue and crime may leave a message about wealth and power; yet one doubts that this is likely to harm the rich or distort the perceptions of the middle class. Link's description of TV is most aptly applied to this series: "TV is an after-dinner mint." The more recent effort of the two men, *Ellery Queen,* is no particular departure from the *Columbo* form, for it offers the same calm, detached puzzle quality with a touch of humor. These two police stories cannot be categorized as violent in the traditional sense, and it is unlikely that lessons are taught or morals imparted, though law does always triumph. The environment does allow the two talented artists, Link and Levinson, full range for setting a liberal tone. Columbo shows tolerance for outsiders. He believes evil should be punished, but he is not judgmental. Columbo, the meat-and-potatoes cop, defeats the very rich and sophisticated.

Baretta

Baretta is something of a surprising success, coming to the air almost accidentally. In January of 1976 it remained in the list of top thirty shows by Nielsen rating. It is a gold mine of preachments and moral admonitions. The hero, played by Robert Blake, is sympathetic to persons in trouble and conveys a warmth and personal concern that is probably appealing to a large segment of the younger population. Baretta cares. Nevertheless, one producer who is identified with quite violent police drama described *Baretta* as a "sick show," irrational, with Blake playing the cop "like a crazy man." The same individual saw "grave danger in kids identifying" with Baretta.

No doubt, *Baretta* is bizarre. A chief ingredient of most plots and an apparent positive assumption is the acceptability of middle-level crime as "cool." In most cases not only are Baretta's informants outside the law, they are his friends on the street, good-hearted, small-time crooks. The underlying justifications for this moral position are quite clearly the inequities of society which have created a world where some crime must be tolerated. In a curious fashion, crime in this series is the reverse of white-collar crime with its country club prisons.

For Baretta the criterion for judging people is the ripple effect created by their crimes. Sometimes he appears to be in league with the small-time criminal to defeat the big-time equivalent (read "murderer") who is giving a bad press to the little man. The ultimate effects of a life of "small-time" crime are not examined, only reduced to short quips in the script. Questions of consequences for persons trapped in the criminal ghetto are only superficially attended. In fact, there seems to be a certain glamour attached to local rackets, prostitution, and gambling. In an effort to avoid moralizing about these activities, the series ignores the human impact on persons caught in this condition. It is, therefore, not an altogether effective social comment, though one expects that is intended. There is, on occasion, an effort made to develop the character of a helpless victim, a child or woman, but the implication is that such a person is thrown once again into the same miserable conditions out of which he or she had been rescued, for a time, by Baretta. The show thus becomes fatalistic.

Baretta himself appears to be a kind of combination of John Garfield and James Dean. The message of this series is not law and order, but the injustice and corruption of society. The hero is constantly reminded that "there, but for the grace of God, go I." He is a young father figure, wisely weaving a pattern of existence for himself and those for whom he cares. He is a product of the environment in which he works, and he understands the people. The law, for him, is a means to helping, but it also may become a means of revenge against those who allegedly create the conditions of poverty and misery, the powerful felons. Baretta hates more vigorously than most TV cops, and he has more immediate empathy than his contemporaries, with the possible exception of Kojak. Baretta, like Garfield, is a victim of the system, but *he* is winning. Like Dean, he is a rebel, but *with* a cause. He is a Dean with the conscience of a Garfield.

The moral content of the series is often cloudy, although in almost every episode there is dramatic evidence of concern for the deprived. The maverick cop, a product of the streets, is compassionate. He comprehends people's problems. It is, however, the dark side of Baretta's personality that probably offends or disturbs many. There is an easy violence connected with the foreknowledge of guilt. In most of the plots, twelve of eighteen analyzed, homicide was a chief ingredient. Baretta's response to murder is violent though always just short of outright mayhem. The theme of the show is pragmatic moralizing, "if you can't do the time, don't do the crime," an update of "crime does not pay."

The moral dilemma for the viewer in all this arises when one queries the impact of a cop who believes in pragmatic justice and then beats the system, breaks the rules, beats his suspects, preaches justice, enforces the law, and encourages small-time crime. It is a bundle of contradictions. But then the writers of this series may well remind us that so is the world in which we live. One might recall President Ford who pardoned Nixon for all his crimes and then saw a person who threatened the President's life receive life imprisonment. Is that any less a condoning of crime followed by strict enforcement of the law?

The violent response of Baretta to "big-time" crime and

mayhem points to an interesting flaw in TV police drama, no matter how realistic such programs appear. Justice, so significant in American law, is irrelevant in police shows. The captured villain is not tried in court. The audience is fully aware of guilt, so who needs a trial? The courtroom, the natural ally and follow-up to police work, is almost totally absent from police drama.[9]

In nearly all cases the audience sees the crime committed or is privy to who did it. In the mind of the viewer a court scene would be superfluous. By the same token violence takes on a different connotation on TV. Since the audience knows beyond doubt, often as eye witnesses, that an accused is guilty, it becomes legitimate for the TV policeman to assume that guilt and, on occasion, knock the individual around or use illegal means of entrapment. A jury is unnecessary because Baretta and his fellow cops on other shows are the jury. The effect is reinforced sympathy for violence by the police in real life, forgetting that the whole system of justice assumes innocence until guilt is proven. This false image of police function could lead to outcries from the public for rejection of the Miranda decision.

Alan Alda posed an interesting question last summer when he inquired, "What would happen if you tried to show police shaking somebody who the audience knew was innocent?" Of course this is never allowed unless it is made clear that the thrust of the show opposes such action. But that is the just the problem, for as a rule we do not know ahead of time in real life. On TV, righteousness hangs over the heads of heroic policemen as a result of foreknowledge.

Granted all the problems discussed, there is something appealing about this "crazy" cop Baretta who is outraged by injustice; and something frightening, too, about the specter of emulation of Baretta without mature grasp of the problems of society against which he reacts. In a way, the series is the moral dilemma that confronts every citizen.

Hawaii Five-O

A highly successful series that has continued to sustain excellent ratings, *Hawaii Five-O* has come upon difficult times this year. The new producer, Philip Leacock, observed last year that "you have to be very careful when you have a very successful show that you don't mess it up." Nevertheless, Leacock has made an effort to humanize Steve McGarrett and to make the entire show more character-oriented. It was Leacock's opinion that *Five-O* had much more interesting character relationships in earlier years, and he was apparently seeking to restore that. CBS may have recognized this new quality because it has once again renewed this well-polished work which began in 1968.

This series has been more regularly criticized for gratuitous violence than most other action programs on TV. Of it the National Association for Better Broadcasting said in 1974: "A very bad show for youngsters of all ages, strategically scheduled to lure a very large youth audience. Graphic horror. Such things as a close-up on a girl as she dies horribly from bubonic plague. A man brutally spits on his attacker to give him the plague . . . and then there are rats, etc." [10] Horace Newcomb speaks of the "vicious world" of *Hawaii Five-O*. [11]

Leacock, an intelligent and cultured Englishman, has been involved in shows as disparate as *The Waltons*, *The New Land*, *Mod Squad*, *The Rookies*, and *Gunsmoke*. As a director and producer he has had an enormously wide range of experience. It is his opinion that *Five-O* tends to be rather moralistic. In answer to critics he responds that he and Jack Lord both decry gratuitous violence. He further notes that the show adheres to the letter of the law. McGarrett may be lenient with offenders whom he believes can be reclaimed, but if guilty of stealing the persons involved must pay the penalty. He and Lord both believe in prohibition of hand guns. Leacock insists that if a script is offensive to him he will "bow out." It must represent his values. And he contends you cannot do anything on TV that is "morally reprehensible."

Leacock does have considerable to say about the censors and scientists who populate the TV industry. He thinks the network "censors" are established to "placate the pressure from outside," and he views social scientists as parasites who make their living on the very things they condemn. Social scientists and psychologists are "dangerous to the arts as well as the TV industry," he says. In describing his responsibilities Leacock was quick to say that "our work is being very much affected by the pressure from the social scientists who are doing the research into effects of violence." Do the network "program practices" people go over the scripts carefully? "Oh my God, yes!" he says.

Leacock believes the networks have substituted measuring devices for good taste, but he contends, "You've got to rely on your own taste in every aspect of this industry." Let the series speak for itself. Since the change in program production has been recent it seemed wise to restrict comment to the episodes that have appeared over the past twelve months.

The charge that *Hawaii Five-O* details the consequences of violence might prove significant. Leacock properly noted that "when a guy is hit by a .45 bullet you should see what it does. You should not have a cut away to something else." Indeed, that is exactly what most police shows do. But the dilemma is real. If you are to employ violence, how much blood is in good taste? To suggest that it is better for a child to see only the act, not the results, may be questionable, to say the least. David Webster of the British Broadcasting Company feels rather strongly that herein lies one of the major differences between British and American TV. He points out that the world is not fair, not just, and that the lack of complexity of character leads to lack of reality. A major contributing factor is that American TV violence does not show consequences. A contrary view expressed by Link and Levinson is that "the new directors . . . rationalize that rubbing the audience's face in violence is going to turn that audience from violence; rather a specious argument we think."

Hawaii Five-O is conditioned by the expansive ego of the star. Not only criminals, but other police officers, citizens, politicians appear as subordinate to McGarrett. The unquestioned loyalty displayed by his men is repaid in protective fatherly stroking. Hence the task which Leacock undertook was a monumental one, that is, to humanize McGarrett. The show combines the puzzle aspects of *Columbo* with the realism of *Kojak*. One of the unique features of this series is its location. Often the police work involves sealing off the islands or in other ways utilizing the isolated nature of the state.

In one respect, the show is a throwback to the early spy genre. Frequently, as in the opening episode for 1975, federal relations enter into the plot. In past seasons these plots have tended to focus on the conflict between East and West, communism and democracy. In more recent episodes this aspect has begun to fade. Ethnic differences are presented in a way to inform the viewer of the polyculture of Hawaii, but the primary burden for law and order falls to non-Orientals. Plot structure guarantees that orders will be given only by McGarrett, and the result is a

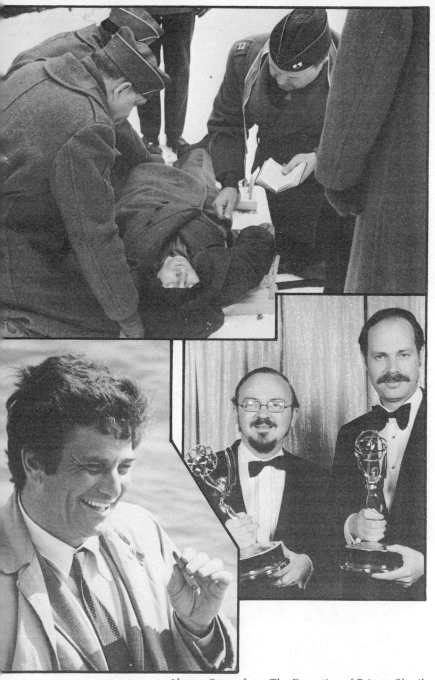

Above: Scene from *The Execution of Private Slovik*
Below, left: Peter Falk as Columbo
Below, right: William Link and Richard Levinson, TV producers

Norman Lear

Clockwise from upper left: The casts of *Maude; The Jeffersons; All in the Family; Mary Hartman, Mary Hartman; Good Times; One Day at a Time*

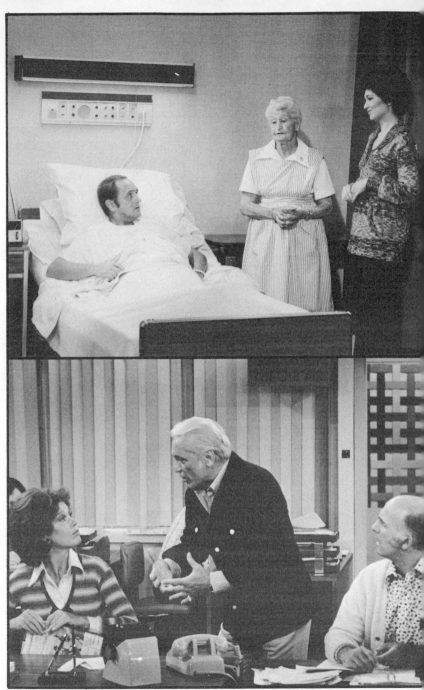

Above: Scene from *The Bob Newhart Show*
Below: Scene from *The Mary Tyler Moore Show*

Earl Hamner (center left) and cast members of The Waltons

Above: Scene from *M*A*S*H**
Below: Author in interview with Alan Alda
    Photo by John R. Alley

Above: Scene from *Streets of San Francisco*
Below: Liam O'Brien, executive producer of *Police Story*

Above: Nancy Malone, vice-president of Twentieth Century-Fox
Below: Cast of *Little House on the Prairie*

picture of subservient non-Westerners. By the same token, women are presented in traditional roles which tend to confirm the "machismo" of the star. In a nicely phrased description, James Cheseboro and Caroline Hamsher made the point: "The romantic hero is part of a legend and possesses a chivalric love for others. There is a supernatural aura essential to romance, and correspondingly the romantic hero appears adventurous, mysterious, and all-knowing." [12]

Youths "lured" to this show are exposed to a diet of law and order where the police almost never bend the rules. Over the several years of its life, *Hawaii Five-O* has been strong in its emphasis upon the virtue of Americanism. The Puritan ethic of hard work and diligence is rewarded with success. The series implies a strict caste system in which even McGarrett knows his place. Governors and other high officials are skillfully woven into plots as persons of the upper class. And everyone follows orders. The dialogue is literate if heavily weighted with traditional ideas such as extreme sexism. This is a man's world into which McGarrett invites us at the conclusion of each episode. Leacock feels they "occasionally do make a point," but for the most part this is straight police entertainment. As such, given its assumptions, it seems no worse and far superior to many others in quality.

One final note on violence. The matter of taste is highly significant when one is commenting upon the appropriateness of scenes of aggression. This series is more explicit respecting violence. It does not follow the guideline that if murder is to be a topic of entertainment, it should be made to appear antiseptic. The chief question for public debate is whether American penchant for violent acts justifies the enormous expansion of such acts on TV.

Kojak

Kojak is the latest in a series of programs that have become identified with a time slot and have proved tremendously successful. Sunday night belongs to *Kojak* and CBS. Once a month *Columbo* may offer a challenge, but Telly Savalas has imbued the character with such style that he is the most prominent dramatic personality currently on the TV screen. Created by Abby Mann, who also sought to blaze significant trails with *Medical Story* (see chapter 4), this series has created a mythic hero for young and old alike.

Lieutenant Theo Kojak, Greek and proud of the heritage, is not only a policeman, he is a sage, a priest of sorts. In a 1974 episode that featured five murders and ten shootings the dialogue was laced with religious allusion. The criminals talked about a listening God and Christian morals. Kojak commented about the Pope and the Church before delivering a closing line to a woman adversary, "Get thee to a convent! *Pax vobiscum*, baby!"

Kojak performs his responsibilities for the New York Police Department in a fantasy world that allows him to range widely over the city. In the early years of the series the officers who surrounded him might have been refugees from the cast of *Barney Miller*. For the most part they were buffoons, incapable of intelligent action save at the direction of the wise and perceptive leader. Recently that has been altered. The image of the dumb flatfoot, so much a staple of the early movie comedies, has been radically shifted to allow a greater emphasis upon team solution to crime. Kojak's acquaintances seem regularly fortuitous and unlikely. He is well acquainted with high crime personalities in the city and treats them as business competitors to be bested in the lists of street combat. With all his sense of justice and fair play he can still be callous.

Commenting upon the murder of an apparent derelict he said to his subordinate: "So some loser gets his ticket punched. What's the big deal?" It becomes a "big deal" only when Kojak discovers the dead man was an undercover cop. Certainly it must be true that a big city policeman becomes somewhat immune to normal human responses to death, which is a constant factor in his work. Nevertheless, the attitude portrayed by his words suggests a perspective that will not contribute to a totally positive view of police work. Or else it may propose an insensitive response to "losers." While Kojak often is deeply concerned over people, his feelings are nowhere so intense as Baretta's.

Several *Kojak* episodes have dealt with problems involving federal agents. Whenever this occurs, Kojak has few kind words for the bureaucracy, which he feels inhibits his work. The federal agents are painted as unfeeling and ambitious men. In one sequence the government agents deliberately endanger an informant in order to play a political game. The result is death for the informant and anger from Kojak. The message is clear. Corruption lies at the federal level, not at the local police level. This value judgment is constantly reinforced, and no matter how valid it may prove to be in a given circumstance, it needs to be noted.

Benjamin Stein, former arts editor of the *Wall Street Journal*, wrote a piece for "News Watch" in *TV Guide* in May of 1975 in which he called on Kojak to keep winning for society's sake. Stein takes as demonstrable that TV drama is influencing morality among viewers, sees Kojak as a "very decent, law-abiding guy whom we like and would like to imitate," and so is pleased that Kojak wins. Since he always does win, the implication is that the law always wins. "It means that moral, kind behavior always wins. It means that justice is done and that the forces defending society triumph over those attacking society." [13] A casual viewer of *Kojak* may have difficulty relating such words as "moral," "kind," and "justice" to the plots of this series. An example from a *Kojak* script would be beneficial. Unfortunately, Universal Studios, which owns the legal rights to the show, refused to grant permission to reprint twenty lines of dialogue from a *Kojak* episode probably viewed by over 20 million persons. While we are inclined to believe that such a brief excerpt from a program broadcast over public channels can be considered fair use when employed for purposes of critical analysis, we will honor the wishes of Universal and seek to do justice to the dialogue through a paraphrase.

This particular show opened with Kojak entering an apartment with a warrant to search for jewels. Unable to discover them, the detective resorted to an arrest based on the possession of a concealed weapon, a kitchen instrument resembling an ice pick. The D.A., angered by the "quick cover-up collar," chastised Kojak for dreaming up a case. He said Kojak had no "right to toy with the law." Kojak's response was bitter. He asked the D.A. whose side he was on and suggested that he "get back to reality." "Pick a side," Kojak cried, as he admitted stretching the law. He noted that perhaps it should be stretched "in the reverse" once in a while. He concluded with an emotional appeal for the D.A. to "come into my courthouse one night"—the streets. Later in the episode the D.A. was painted as the heavy and the script's depiction of murder and other felonious acts exonerated Kojak's actions and indignation. The message was unmistakable: The D.A. was living in an unreal world that aided crime.

What has been described is a typical problem. Rough and illegal behavior by police is tolerated because of known guilt. Courts are an impairment. If Stein is correct about moral influence, the signals emitted by this specific episode could hardly sustain justice and a system of law predicated upon proof of guilt. It is extremely easy to take shots at legal procedure when the cards are stacked against the defender of that system. Why not bend the law this once? We know he's guilty. Kojak is symbolic of the genre in this respect, and because of his enormous popularity, he is a primary source of concern. Violence in this show is not guns alone, for it often involves violence to a precious judicial tradition.

Returning to Kojak's Greek heritage, no less an authority on ethnic cultures than Michael Novak says, "The accents, gestures, methods, and perceptions of the leading actors in *Kojak* reflect in an interesting and accurate way the ethnic sensibilities of several neighborhoods in New York."[15] As the series has grown, this ethnicity has somewhat diminished, and, while Kojak is still Greek, his identity now comes to the viewer as a function of his personality. In the process of becoming the star of Sunday evening his subculture has lost significance. Kojak does things now because he is Lieutenant Kojak, not because he is Greek. Nonetheless, it has been a nice touch and has contributed to overall effectiveness of the series. The drama, like many others, is well produced and acted. It is entertaining but biased in several directions that should not be ignored.

Having explored six ways in which TV relays an image of the police to the public, it is appropriate to return to a common denominator with which we began and to establish those conclusions about police and detective dramas which appear satisfactory in light of the evidence. Conclusions will relate not alone to the six series which have been described as representative.

An interesting aspect of the 1972 Surgeon General's report on TV violence was its support for nearly every position on the issue. Recognizing this handicap, it still appears appropriate to note some pertinent remarks on "Parental Emphasis on Nonaggression." Discussing the impact of such emphasis the study concluded:

> Parental emphasis on nonaggression emerged as a strong candidate for a third variable. Where such emphasis is low, the relationship between violence viewing and aggression occurs; where it is high, the relationship is markedly reduced. This finding is consonant with the earlier mentioned finding of Dominick and Greenberg, to the effect that family attitudes regarding violence are more strongly related to aggressive attitudes than is violence viewing for fourth-to-sixth-grade boys and girls. Taken together, the two findings strongly underscore the need for more extensive inquiry into the role which pertinent family attitudes play in the relationship between violence viewing and aggression.[16]

Reviewing our discussion of police-detective shows supports certain conclusions. (1) TV reinforces the commonly received attitudes about aggression. There is little argument that there is an excessive amount of violence on TV, although we have indicated how most of it might be avoided even by heavy viewers. But apart from the suggested nonviolent schedule, parental attitudes appear highly significant. In technical language, "the average correlation (between violence viewing and all measures of aggression in both of the samples) is .26 in families where little stress is placed upon nonaggression; in families where such emphasis is found, the average correlation is only .07."[17]

Parents who emphasize competition and aggressive response to child experiences are here lumped with the vast middle group who passively accept violent solutions to conflict as necessary. Our society categorizes as "sissy" those boys who respond to conflict by other than aggressive means. This has been true much longer than the existence of television. Ironically, it can be effectively argued that the parent who seriously emphasizes nonaggression as a precept is rearing a child probably far more capable of expressing convictions and standing for his beliefs. In fact, the environment that encourages physical aggression is much more conforming to outmoded social mores or taboos defining success. Alan Alda highlights the problem effectively in the following comment:

> A very big problem as a nation, as a culture, has been the idea that success in life equals monetary success and that aggression is always at someone's expense, that you only succeed through someone else's loss, that cooperation is the antithesis of competition . . . the unspoken assumption that if you squeeze the last drop out of somebody then you have made a good deal is a value that is not doing us any good as a group.

Evidence appears to support the proposition that where violence on TV reinforces violence-prone home attitudes, greater aggression may result. Simply stated, TV intensifies prevailing conditions. Further, until such time as a majority of American homes actively pursue nonaggression, the models on television will accurately reflect prevailing cultures.

(2) The study of police-detective programs indicates that violence is present in fairly large doses. While it is usually shielded from the viewers' full awareness, *Hawaii Five-O* tends to more realism. However, almost all shows investigated justified violence only where it was performed in pursuit of "good" goals, normally by the police. Private detective shows err with fair regularity by setting the hero as far outside the law as the criminal. *Mannix*

traded on gratuitous violence in which the hero was justified in his acts on the ground of prior aggressive acts upon him or his client. Retribution is less a factor in straight police drama.

Historically, Americans have dealt with violence in terms of justified retaliation. Like a sleeping giant possessing a great stick, violence was a secure weapon in the name of retributive justice. From the Alamo to the *Maine* to the *Lusitania* to Pearl Harbor to the Gulf of Tonkin, our nation has judged violence primarily by the standard of who acted first. This form of the just war theory has allowed small concern over the more subtle causes of conflict or how violence might have been avoided. Until Americans challenge this national perception TV will continue to reflect it. Vietnam came close to raising this issue, but the time has passed. An illustration of this point may be observed in a news report on NBC TV in 1964. In the summer there had been devastating floods in Vietnam, killing people and destroying crops in the south. The commentator, after sadly reporting the tragedies, offered the thought that there was only one good effect of the flood: several dozen Vietcong were killed. In essence, the enemies' lives are cheap. Transferred to criminal enemies, this tends to appear equally valid. The remarks of Alan Alda given at the beginning of this chapter are pertinent.

(3) The twenty-five years of TV may have informed us that there is a large market for retributive violence, Western or police. If saturation has presently been achieved, it may not provide helpful clues for the future. Nevertheless, the Nielsen ratings tend to support the idea that nonviolent shows are currently more popular. Sensing this trend, NBC announced in January of 1976 that they "are de-emphasizing police and detective shows in our '76-'77 plans." Vice-president Frank Barton stressed

that "comedy is really the whole posture at CBS." [18] Interestingly, 1976 midseason replacements included *Jigsaw John, City of Angels,* and *The Blue Knight*—all police-oriented.

It seems a safe bet that public response to more and more comedies will be negative. Since the networks' imaginations seem locked to three professions—doctor, lawyer, law-enforcer—the return of a previously successful genre cannot be discounted. Unless, heaven forbid, the January 15 headline in the *Hollywood Reporter* proves prophetic: "Nets Mull Bringing Back Prime Time Game Shows" (p. 3).

(4) Attacks on TV violence by well-meaning groups have been largely erratic and without focus. No real discrimination is regularly employed in inquiring into the nature of individual programs and their intention. Profit motive is always assumed to preclude intelligent conversation, leading to calls for government action or citizen boycott. Counting acts of violence may become ludicrous and produce an overreaction leading to demands for censorship. A more positive recent effort, the Humanitas Prize, is designed to cite TV writers of scripts that portray humanity with sensitivity, dignity, compassion, and hope. An effort spearheaded by James A. Brown, S.J., it seeks to encourage humanistic values in television. But the same James Brown also points out:

> We should reflect on more than 2,000 years of staged drama, and consider how many theatrical plays of those centuries we even know, much less care about or read or stage in our own time. We can recall that of 8,000 plays copyrighted each year and recorded in the Library of Congress, only 80 plays are produced (for highly selective audiences) annually on or near Broadway, of which 15 to 20 may be moderately successful. We must therefore wonder at the enormity of the challenge to broadcast managers to program quality content

to the total national audience of 210 million people 365 days a year. The fact that the medium produces several outstanding multi-hour presentations a month deserves more praise than the meager annual productivity of Broadway.[19]

As long as the networks insist upon flooding the airwaves with over fifteen police-detective dramas in a season, the results are likely to prove disastrous. Quality will vary and content will either be repetitive or bizarre, as witness *S.W.A.T.* The maudlin sentimentality of *Bronk* when a middle-aged cop has to kill his own son is enough to convince the viewer that quality is not always a concern of the producer.

There does not appear to be a major correlation between the political events of 1968-70 and the TV police shows. From the Democratic Convention in Chicago to John Mitchell, the nation was treated to a bombardment of negative reaction to police. President Nixon called a conference on the subject of TV influence, which resulted in a brief stint for a series on the Treasury Department. Certainly programs such as *The Streets of San Francisco, The Rookies, Police Story,* and *Kojak* seek to project a positive image of the police, and Aaron Spelling believes it is the only positive projection most persons in a ghetto like Watts receive. Robert T. Howard, president of the NBC television network, believes that "television is contributing to greater public understanding and acceptance of the role of the police and the judiciary." Just how the judicial system is being exposed to the public was not made clear. In fact, his address to the annual meeting of the Citizens for Law Enforcement Needs in Los Angeles sounded more like a promotion of the NBC schedule. He did observe that it is "not television's role to propose any particular solution to society's ills."[20] This raises the question of whether television has the responsibility to make available exposure to novel ideas so that better solutions might be discovered. David Webster of the BBC was musing on this issue during the summer of 1975 when he commented that he often wondered whether the BBC's decisions on news from Northern Ireland between 1950 and 1968 might have contributed to the bloody conditions that now prevail. He suggested there had been a failure to deal realistically with Ireland.

The most disturbing fact about the 1976 winter schedule of the three networks was the paucity of drama beyond the crime genre. Apart from two medical shows, the number was four: *Movin' On*, the network's nod to the blue-collar worker, *Swiss Family Robinson*, an ill-contrived, if currently popular adventure, *The Waltons*, and *Little House on the Prairie*. Since the demise of the various anthologies the situation has been similar year after year. Presumably this was corrected to some degree by specials that dot the scene. The 1976-77 season suggests some attention to this problem with the episodic character of shows like *Rich Man, Poor Man* and *Family* joined by *Best Sellers*.

NEW DIRECTIONS IN SERIES DRAMA

The Waltons

One of the most interesting phenomena of the seventies has been the sustained success of *The Waltons*, followed by the equally distinctive *Little House on the Prairie*. As of December, 1975, the former was in eighth position among all shows rated between September 8 and December 21. *Little House* was in fourteenth position. Earl Hamner, creator of *The Waltons*, noted in commenting about his success, "There is a myth in the networks that shows with rural settings won't sell." When one considers that Nielsen rates only the 70 percent of the population in major metropolitan areas, the actual rating of the *Waltons* may be staggering.

The most obvious thing about *The Waltons* is its morality. It is rife with old-fashioned virtues. Cynics have been wont to suggest that Hamner's life in rural Virginia was surely not as idyllic as painted, but the same may be said of most dramatic fiction. What has been captured is a life perceived by people of another era as being ideal. It is romanticized memory based upon life as it might have been, though perhaps really never was. Yet it has the ring of reality. At least one reason could be the complex nature of the storytelling. While Hamner orders the scripts to reflect the point of view of John-Boy, what emerges is a perception of life as envisioned by the grandfather. With a blending of his own past and an openness to the future, the old gentleman, observing the forward flow of his family, is the storyteller. In this manner the stories become essentially projections of hopes and dreams rather than simple reflections on times gone by. For that reason, because it is forward-looking, the series has currency. And largely because it is the grandfather, ably played by Will Geer, who sets this tone, a potentially narrow vision on morality never quite materializes.

The Waltons is not really predictable. Hamner perceives this in saying that he "keeps away from what an audience might expect of us." I have discussed the series with many persons who have said they sometimes hesitate to watch *The Waltons* because of an anticipated sermon, but they invariably come away pleased from nearly every episode. While some of this effective dramatic impact must be credited to a sterling cast and a remarkable creator, it also relates to the fact that *The Waltons* is not really so conservative on personal morality or religion as one continually expects it to be. Rather than looking back to a "better" day, the plots usually center around projections of the family into the future, the unknown, thereby providing far greater realism than would simple reminiscense.

This effect is all the more remarkable when one remembers the moral assumptions incorporated into all scripts. John-Boy reminds viewers, through the stirring voice of Earl Hamner, of the values inherent in each plot, "values that were taught to me as a child by my family in Virginia."

> Out of that "breakdown" my brother emerged with a new maturity and he and I came to a better understanding. We stopped the old game of "Follow the Leader" and began to face things together—side by side.
>
> I was never again to stand in for Reverend Fordwick. But it was an humbling experience and a growing time. One that I learned much from and have occasion to recall—all the days of my life.
>
> Lyle Thomason came back to stay with us several more times, and we enjoyed his visits very much. He did indeed prove to be a decent, kind, and very likable human being. But what pleased us even more was that after that weekend Lyle spent almost all of his free time in Emporia visiting his own parents.[21]

Morals indeed abound. The maturing of siblings, their appropriate adjustments, the value of lessons from difficult experiences, the quality of kindness, the place of the home in the life of growing children—all of these receive dramatic focus intentionally. The family is the rock of dependability. This is nowhere better illustrated than in a comment about his mother uttered by John-Boy, "Still, we knew she was there—watching—waiting—ready to help if ever . . . whenever we reached out."

Virtues of hard work, diligence, honesty, as Hamner puts it "pioneer virtues of thrift, industry, self-reliance, faith in God, trust in man, the Golden Rule," these are the stuff of *Waltons* plots. In a unique fashion Hamner has been able to convey such virtues without too large a dose of syrup. The popular nature of the series and the respect exhibited by professional colleagues (two Emmy awards in 1976) are testimony to this fact. The magic did not always work with *Apple's Way*. It exuded morality as a means of attracting an audience. While most of the moralizing was politically and socially liberal, the show was weighted with old-fashioned virtues that occasionally tended to put off some who might have agreed with the ideas. The series was interesting, and with its nostalgic packaging coupled with quite obvious messages, it was something of a television departure. Mr. Apple, the enlightened citizen, dealt weekly with "narrow-minded people on the narrow-minded street where he lived." Apple tried a little kindness which encouraged businessmen and politicians to melt into decent types. There was almost a revival flavor to the hour. In marked contrast with *The Waltons*, *Apple's Way* had a contemporary setting, which raises an interesting speculative question. Can a continuing series deal with a family setting that is contemporary without making it comedic or raunchy? If one shows a modern family, reality becomes a problem because, while accuracy may be demanded, the members of most families have too many tensions to want them reflected. In part, that may have doomed Alda's efforts in *We'll Get By*.

Reflecting on *Apple's Way*, Hamner has no regrets about the series but feels the characters could have been humanized and given greater dimension, rather than having to appear either good or bad. Apple had to have an issue a day. This tended to polarize. In the discussion of

Television Drama

this undertaking Hamner noted that time was a factor. The series was requested by the network so quickly that conception and development were nearly impossible. The pressure of time has a telling effect upon quality, a problem addressed in the final chapter, and it was compounded in this instance.

An important ingredient in *The Waltons* is the identification of its creator with the show. Most TV series are, for the vast majority of the audience, anonymous. Few viewers know the names of producers, writers, creators, although they appear weekly on the crawl of credits. If one reads a novel or sees a play, almost invariably the identity of the novelist or playwright is known. Again, the TV writer seldom shepherds his handiwork through to conclusion. Television shows are committee affairs— producers, directors, film editors, actors—quickly hatched and passed by. So Hamner is unusual. He hovers over scripts and story development as well as the long hours of filming. Technical questions about authenticity are regularly referred to him. He is an essential ingredient in the total process.

One comes away from the set of *The Waltons* impressed by a degree of caring by all portions of the company. To be sure, the economic realities are ever-present. Career growth is clearly as much a factor for actors and directors as for professors and lawyers. Salary was an issue for the cast in 1975. Yet these people are not any more one-dimensional than are any other segment of the population. They are concerned for their craft. And, from my vantage point, Hamner provides the glue for the company with his commitment to "affirming attitudes toward people." In translating the affirmative to film, *The Waltons* becomes a conservative setting with traditional dialogue for essentially liberal solutions to problems. It is an excellent balance that sets some rather high standards for the industry.

Little House on the Prairie

A former associate of Earl Hamner now produces *Little House on the Prairie*. John Hawkins generously spent an afternoon with me in early July of 1975. He spoke of TV morals and sponsors and audience response. What follows are excerpts of that conversation which offer thoughtful reflection on an industry by a veteran producer.

There hasn't been any recent sponsor pressure because most shows nowadays are sponsored in a magazine concept. When *Bonanza* was number one the show was totally sponsored by Chevrolet. And Chevrolet used to say that they would like this or they would like that. . . . With the escalating costs, to sponsor one show totally became so vastly expensive the sponsors didn't think it was worthwhile because you got too narrow a segment of the audience you were trying to reach to sell, so it was better to have a minute on ten shows or two minutes on five shows and that way you could pick what you thought was demographically best for you. If you're selling Cadillacs you don't buy a minute of time on *Hee Haw*. This is the demographic situation at its broadest. Try to find a show that appeals to a particular audience. Now with us, when we started, research had the hard-held belief that we were all right except in the area where the most money was—which was the 18-35 group. . . . My feeling was it didn't work that way. This show, I insisted, will be seen in the living room because the mother knows it's a show children can watch . . . no sex, no violence . . . it has a nice moral balance. As soon as parents have watched it for a month, you've got the parents. That's exactly what happened.

There is another show that could be something like *Little*

House if it materializes and that is *Holvak*. . . . It could be a pretty good thing except that they are hitting the moral judgments right on the nose. For example, a man comes to town in a "red-neck" town. This is where the attitude is wrong. When you are talking about red-necks and are producing something about red-necks you have got a distorted view of the people you are talking about. There aren't any red-necks, there are only people. But if you have that attitude you are coming at it on a bias. Anyway, into this town comes a man with a Cadillac. He's bought a house. He's a New York stockbroker. Immediately these people dislike him. The people are down on him until the preacher discovers the man doesn't have anything except the Cadillac, and he has to sell that to buy a team to try to plow, and he doesn't know how to farm. Finally the preacher prevails upon the rest of these Wall Street haters to view this man as not all that bad. But, you see, this kind of meeting of moral judgments squarely is like a train wreck. I don't think you could stand that every week.

In television as in barrooms two things have been kind of outlawed by just general agreement, knowing they can be nothing but trouble—one is religion and the other is politics. Anytime you raise your voice in a political argument in a bar, the next thing you know, you've got a riot. Start talking about religion in bars and the next thing you know the owner is throwing everybody out in the street. He has to, because it gets completely out of hand. Particularly when you mix booze and religion or booze and politics.

His long-running success with *Gunsmoke* and *Bonanza* attest to John Hawkins' savvy as a producer. He is knowledgeable, affable, and thoroughly acquainted with his profession. He knows how to achieve winners. *Little House* is obviously a very dear thing to him and the cast works harmoniously. These people put themselves into the product and the viewers have responded affirmatively. His remarks on the *The Family Holvak* series were perceptive because what I would term the exceedingly pious stance of the show probably undermined its effectiveness. It may not have been so much meeting issues head-on as it was preaching too hard about them. *Apple's Way* tended to succumb to the same malady. The moral preachments cannot be so obvious for, as Alda commented earlier, success is in inverse ratio to the hiddenness of the preaching.

Hawkins does raise the important issue of TV drama's inability to deal with religion and politics. These are human concerns too central to be ignored by mutual agreement. Wise and talented dramatists can find the way to overcome this inhibition, and it is incumbent upon the networks to encourage such variety.

Chapter VI
Humor Is Ethics

It may be possible to extend research to the absurd, and on occasion it appears that such has been the case respecting television portrayals of sex and violence. One of the things upon which all this investigation has focused is a recent national proclivity toward suspicion of new and untried ideas. As a nation we appear conditioned to be suspect of novelty in thought, harboring fears that it will contribute to corruption. Unfortunately, this means that innovative uses of communications media are often suspect. Those motivated by profit came to accept the bland and often debilitating pabulum, so much a staple of TV in the fifties, as safe and normative. Fortunately, in the past six years willingness to encourage some change in that policy has allowed TV comedies to delve somewhat deeper into the American experience. In so doing, the comedies have uncovered levels of concern that require new language and images which, in turn, have conjured up the old bugbear—fear of novel ideas. Hence, TV has once more to struggle with problems of censorship. This is particularly distressing when one comes to perceive that many of the newer representations are significant though unrecognized forms of the prophetic tradition of the Bible.

NORMAN LEAR—MODERN AMERICAN MORALIST

No one, of course, can dismiss Norman Lear. He has, as they say in the business, massive clout. His fingers appear to create gold. *All in the Family, Good Times, Maude, One Day at a Time, Sanford and Son, The Jeffersons,* and *Mary Hartman, Mary Hartman* are tribute not only to his talent but to his popular appeal. Some network executives may not care for the Lear approach (particularly when it brings law suits), but they must respect his success at the "box office" of the industry, the Nielsens.

A window into that executive mind is available to anyone who reads for several days a trade paper like *Variety* or the *Hollywood Reporter*. The emphasis in the advertising is repetitive, forever concerned about how much a particular picture grossed. No one is likely to equate gross with quality either in TV or cinema. But the gross is the thing. And Lear has won at that game while retaining quality.

Who is Norman Lear? Clearly he is a success in his chosen profession. He has been a recognized talent for more than half of television's national years. People who know him have widely divergent reactions to him personally and professionally. In my own experience I found him a concerned, ethically sensitive dramatist with enormous comedic talent.

Our first meeting was quite accidental. I had engaged in a lengthy dialogue with the vice-president of TAT Communications, Virginia Carter. As we were discussing various aspects of Lear's endeavors he walked in. I was preparing to leave, having an unbreakable engagement with a writer of soap operas. Jealously, I pursued the things I most wanted to discuss with Lear. At that juncture he proposed that we meet over the weekend at his home. He volunteered as much time as I wanted. Norman Lear does not need me to be impressed with him, so I concluded then what I still believe, that he felt the area of television and social ethics was of critical importance. In this belief he occupies common ground with a number of his colleagues in the industry, some of whom will be discussed elsewhere in these pages.

I must confess that I find interviewing to be akin to a tourist going to the Soviet Union for a week without any knowledge of the language and returning as a Russian expert. Appearances may be and often are deceiving. In the large number of contacts I made during the months of 1975 and 1976 I am certain that I received my share of PR. However, as Aaron Spelling observed when I raised this point, "I don't have time for that. I have more important things to do than spend time trying to con you." I expect he is right, although a cynic might respond by asking whether that remark was part of the PR act. Who is to know? Finally, the interviewer must make his own assessment, risking the possibility of error. One way to minimize this problem is to examine the work of the individual engaged in dialogue in order to ascertain whether his creative product conforms to his personal self-image.

Norman Lear makes profits, has a considerable ego, and certainly understands public relations, but he is also, in my opinion, quite genuine. His manner is at once both easy and tense. He seems driven by ideas and interest in the human condition. For the television industry he has become something of a paradox. Week after week he produces, by Nielsen standards, the most acceptable TV fare in the mind of the public, and that makes him invaluable to the networks. Yet both network executives and government officials seem prepared to reject his opinions relative to what is good taste for the public.

Possibly the difference between Lear's intention and that of the networks and government lies in the fact that while the former desires to incorporate his impressions of reality into artistic form, the latter wish to impress a form upon the artistic endeavor consistent with presumed public opinion. Lear wants to apply the same standards to TV that are applicable to other communication media, and then to trust public judgment. Network officials appear honestly fearful that public "innocence" will be lost if creativity is allowed too great a freedom. Certainly the quasi-public nature of TV raises legitimate questions about comparisons with other media, but, as we shall seek to show, television has inherent qualities that offer quite adequate "protection" to the citizen.

Occasionally, it seems that network directors are like some clergy. Frequently, ministers, sophisticated in knowledge about their trade, condescend to express only the least controversial material to their congregations. They regularly underestimate their audience. Likewise, there are educational administrators who fear that honest exchange of ideas in the community at large may scar the sensitivities of the "unwashed" and cost their institution some gifts. There is adrift in the nation an elitist mentality, not of the left, but of the moderate middle. After decades, the work of Gallup and Harris may have begun to take its toll. Market analysis and pretesting of selected audiences determine the form most products will assume. The public is dehumanized and polled to death. As might be expected, TV moguls appear to protect the profit motive through fear of ideas, resulting in the production of "preshrunk" evening fare.

It should be noted in fairness, that the commercial networks did provide a platform for Lear's emergence in television, and that was on my mind as we talked for several hours in his New England style home, nestled in a quiet, exclusive area of west Los Angeles. But Lear has not forgotten this fact either and his challenges to the industry should be viewed in the context of the pleasure he experiences in what he is doing. And what he is doing is significant.

The reader may have watched a four-part *Maude* plot aired in September of 1975 in which the star ran, unsuccessfully, for the New York Senate. In July of 1975 the story line for these episodes was incomplete. A bare outline was emerging respecting the resolution of Maude's desire to enter the race and the distress of her husband, but no decision had been reached as to whether she would run. As I listened, Lear and Virginia Carter exchanged strong opinions over what should happen to Maude and Walter, causing the TV characters to jump to life. In the discussion there was a strong concern for accuracy, art, and audience. What was to be done about Walter's alcoholism? How could that be treated without doing violence to the progress made by Alcoholics Anonymous? Again, could the dilemma posed be resolved without doing damage to Maude's witness for women's rights? How could all these various concerns be woven into good drama? For anyone who has wondered how television stories are developed, the following dialogue offers a revealing clue.

> Lear: What's disturbing about Maude running and losing is that it's a wet rag. She's entering a race where the odds are against her. Everybody says it would be wrong to suggest that they weren't; that's the way it is. If she loses there's no drama in it.
> Carter: It is the reality of one's political aspirations, however, that on the first run you are sent to the slaughter. It's how you get your political scars.
> Lear: If it's a drama about politics or its machinations, that is the making of a *Playhouse 90*.
> Carter: Are you sure of that? Maybe there is something to be said for the process of politics, that it is an "upper" instead of a "downer." We go around these days (I do with my friends) saying, "Christ! it's not working, the system is designed to put idiots in office." I have a

nervous feeling about that. Maybe it's so, maybe if one explored the process . . .

Lear: But that's not what this is about. This is about a man and woman, about a male-female problem, at this time, in the seventies. Should she be allowed her thing? To switch it into a political story would be . . .

Carter: It comes back saying that life is a wet rag if when you ask a question, Should she be allowed to do her own thing? the answer is no, and she is the one who will disallow it.

Lear: It's not a wet rag to me if she breaks for any reason, and to save her marriage gives in and her last line is: "It's so unfair."

Carter: That is the same argument though, Norman, as the alcoholic's argument. If she gives up what she wants to save her marriage what she has done is ruin it. She doesn't have any marriage if that's what she has to do. Self-sacrifice at that significant level in a person's aspirations is exceedingly unattractive.

Lear: Well, we might examine the man's situation, too. That's where this marvelous drama exists; exactly the same thing happens to him. If I sell my store because I will not be without her—I would rather be with her and move to Albany—I have taken what I have worked for for thirty years and have chucked it. I have tried to see it her way to a point where I've sacrificed everything. What have I done to our marriage?

Carter: What is the reaction to the other possibility, if Maude says, "I want to do this," and Walter says, "If you do what you want to do you have forced us out of marriage or forced me to sacrifice myself."

Lear: I don't accept those semantics. I won't say if you do what you do, you are breaking the marriage or forcing me to sacrifice. I'll say, "Maude, why are you going to leave me for five days a week, nine months a year?"

Carter: And she's saying, "Because I want to. I've balanced these two things, the five days with you and the political career, and I'm telling you, Walter, I've decided it's a fair trade. I want to live up there, and I'll sacrifice for five days." She's saying that, by saying she wants to run for office. "I am prepared to sacrifice you because I want this other so badly."

Lear: He can't do it.

Carter: When he says, "I can't handle that, you will have to stay home," nothing he can say will get her back because she's already told him, "I've balanced those two things and I've decided I'll sacrifice you. . . ." Any compromise that is total self-sacrifice of one partner for the other is sick.

Lear: I think if we pull it off the best thing we could do for women would not be for her to continue (even if it were the last show and nothing mattered). I'm not sure her running is the best thing for women. I think the best thing for women is to develop the four episodes so that men and women alike want her to run. But for Maude there is just too much left of society's male attitude. There is Walter, who can't give up his thirty years' identity, and Vivian, who thinks Maude's place is with her husband, and a daughter who says, "Mother you have to make your own decisions." Everywhere Maude turns there is no help. If, at the end of four episodes, she caves and says, "It's so unfair, it's so unfair" and 80 percent of men believe it is unfair and 92 percent of women think it's unfair, I think we will have done far better for that point of view than to have had her run and get 40 percent of men to feel, "I'm glad she ran," and no point is made at all.

Carter: I disagree with you strongly. When Maude folds, 80 percent of men are going to think that's precisely what she should have done and 60 percent of women, because women always fold in the crunch. They are the ones who sacrifice. In the stresses and strains between men and women in marriages, when career aspirations are on the line, the women always fold! They are told to.

Lear: I understand that, but it would be a first if any amount of men were sorry for it. If they saw it mirrored and were sorry.

Carter: How would we all feel towards Maude forevermore? As a stranger, coming to the show, watching it happen, I'll think my symbol of strong independent womanhood just caved before my very eyes!

Lear: Your symbol of strong independent womanhood is already too strong for many of your feminist friends and not strong enough for others. There is no way you make it work for everybody.

[Question: How does Walter's alcoholism affect the plot?]

Carter: The alcohol people say that neither spouse should make an act of self-sacrifice in an effort to be helpful or support the individual who is the alcoholic. That being the case [neither one should make an act of self-sacrifice] . . . what the alcohol people say is that when you are married to an alcoholic you should detach with love. There is no other way to bring the problem to focus. So it cannot be alcoholism around which this play revolves in the final analysis, or we will be sending the wrong message. As to whether it's a feminist question or not, I cannot conceive of a television program in which the man aspiring to high office chooses not to run because his wife wants him to stay home. But put all that aside too, and then ask the question "Where are we in 1975?" We're at a point when for the first time in the history of this country significant numbers of women are running for state and local office.

Lear: Well, it's a sensational group of dynamics, I tell you. It's just marvelous to have those dynamics to work with. I'm not so concerned about the impact we're having because I don't know about that. I'm concerned for what it is we're delivering for whatever impact it may have. It doesn't make any sense to me to do a story and inadvertently, for all the people suffering with the problem, do the problem of alcoholism a disservice. By the same token, for all the women who need the help and the men who need the help, because, frankly, I am convinced the whole move-ment is going to help men as much as its going to help women, I would hate to, for lack of foresight or thought,

with no knowledge of what the impact is going to be, to
fail to deliver a sensible reason for the plot.

For anyone who saw the final product the effect of this
conversation is obvious. Something of a compromise was
struck in which Maude did run, but by an effective
concluding scene the drama was retained. In a last-minute
TV appearance Maude took a stand for freedom that
brought her from landslide defeat to a close loss. Politics
was an "upper" and the entire four episodes were far from
a wet rag.

It is, I believe, proper to conclude, after constant
viewing of his work over several seasons, that Norman
Lear fills the role of an American moralist. If the medium
of TV is as potent and powerful as most observers now
believe, he holds a position of preeminence. He has
emerged through a complex of television offerings as a
sharp commentator on the American scene. Accepting the
principle that humor is ethics, he has contributed a
plethora of folk heroes to our current culture. From Archie
to Florida they have become household names. And now,
as Lear enters the world of educational TV and daytime
programming, his figure looms ever larger. Feared by
many, resented by more, idolized by a few, he is judged
weekly by millions. Shepherding scripts and meeting
audiences, he and his associates are, as it is said, doing
well. What are they doing well?

Turning from producer to product, the new wave of
comedy calls for close scrutiny. Due to the subjects
considered by *All in the Family*, that series early became a
focus for analysis and criticism. It was suspect from the
beginning in the eyes of the *New York Times* which
wrote, "none of this is funny." *Life* noted it as "a wretched
program" and California *Variety* commented upon it as a
"raw, plotless wonder." On the other coast, New York

Variety saw it as the best comedy since *Bilko.* Lear took out an ad in the trade papers and printed the two *Variety* reviews, highlighting the controversial nature of the show.

For six years now the moral thrust of this series has been dissected by observers. Spencer Marsh published a brief volume in 1975 which attempted a theological analysis, character by character. While Marsh may have been on the mark in identifying Mike, the son-in-law, as the true believer in justice and morality, unfortunately he finds it necessary to fall into the religious stereotype of informing Mike: "He [Jesus] inspires us, empowers us, and leads us to share the Good News of life that is available to all. You would like him, Mike!" [1] But that is a large part of the problem faced by Gloria and Mike. They have had their fill of pious ministerial pronouncements suggesting a paternalistic attitude toward those who fail to enunciate the faith in traditional churchly formulas. It is idle to assert that rebels do not "know Jesus." Accused of rebelling against the faith, Hadrian VII responded to his critic, "I am not in revolt against the faith, I am in revolt against the faithful." In spite of this tendency to describe the faith in propositional terms, Marsh does offer some interesting insights that make his book worth reading. Other writers have been less charitable to Archie, claiming the show "encourages bigots to excuse and rationalize their own prejudices." [2]

The Lear family of comedies reflects a remarkable respect for monogomy, marital fidelity, and family unity. While humor at the expense of these concepts is frequent, the overriding message supports a traditional view. With all the strife in the Bunker household, the daughter, in her twenties, has remained at home. Even though economics may have demanded that Mike and Gloria live with her parents while he was in school, when they moved into their own home, it was next door. That was a highly traditional act, consistent with behavior of persons with an intense sense of family solidarity. And what kind of family structure will Mike and Gloria establish? Well, they may have experimented with sex before marriage, but fidelity is central, and their child is clearly to be reared with the ever-present care of Edith and Archie. Loving each other, the young couple create a foundation for family unity.*

As one turns to the other series the same observations apply. Lamont lives with his widowed father, Fred Sanford, and the loyalty to each other is never lost even at the height of the vaudeville atmosphere and generation gap humor. Maude, married four times, retains strong commitment to an ideal for herself and her daughter, Carol. Divorce is reality, marriage is the ideal. Walter and

* A particularly interesting comedic rendering are Carol Burnett's skits on the family which have become a staple part of her show in recent years. Remarkably well acted by Burnett, Harvey Korman, and Vicki Lawrence, the setting is southern and low-income. While the values examined and proffered in *All in the Family* are generally identifiable, the same cannot be affirmed of the frequent episodes on the Burnett show. In spite of the humor and consequent laughter, there is an underlying bitterness, unrelenting and unresolved. These are unhappy people, trapped with each other. Ed, who could perhaps be content with "Bowling for Dollars" and his small business, is regularly disrupted by the unattainable ambitions of his wife and the bitter resentments of the mother-in-law. Anger affects relationships with friends, children, and each other. Whether this sketch is intended as a caricature of *All in the Family* or a comic rendering of Willy Loman, it raises some serious questions concerning the role of comedy on TV. The pathos and frustrations of life will be familiar to millions, but the thought lingers that the "slapstick" humor is somehow incongruous with the serious nature of the fare. The Burnett characters are closely identified with a particular culture and are strikingly provincial. For these reasons the format may be incapable of bearing the weight of moral freight inherent in the dialogue. In any event, it is a most ambitious undertaking and worthy of scrutiny.

Maude love vigorously, violently. And here again the daughter lives with the mother and everyone cares for Carol's son. Some of the most warming moments have been between Phillip and Walter (grampa).

The Jeffersons have a grown son, Lionel, still honoring his family with whom he lives. Three generations clash in a family setting, a protective environment where the world seems at arm's length. Ann Romano of *One Day At A Time* is divorced, but the maintenance of the family is central to the plot. The two girls struggle with freedom in their maturing years, but they remain loyal to each other and to their mother. The family unit is so important to Ann that she fears marriage again because she has been hurt. She will not gamble her life or her family's happiness on the possibility of a second mistake.

Good Times pits the family unit against external forces of crime, drugs, and injustice which threaten in a ghetto existence. Two teenagers are totally accepting of patriarchial authority. When the son J.J. challenges that authority he ends in distress, eloping with a young girl hooked on hard drugs. Shining through the drama is the unmistakable message that the family is the bedrock of society, a necessary concomitant of survival, a theme heightened by the father's death in the first episode of 1976-77. Even *Mary Hartman, Mary Hartman,* as it satirizes daytime TV, develops a great deal more sense of family solidarity than is found in the average soap opera.

Within the family context Lear goes to work with his essentially liberating ideals, including respect for variant ideas. "Traditional" families would normally not tolerate the level of disagreement and discussion which occurs in most TAT productions. Challenges to accepted moral views and religious affiliations are and have been causes for conflict, but they do not, for Lear, produce a permanent fracture of relations. The family is the one

136

place where understanding can be achieved, even following violent disagreement. That is Lear's interpretation of what family means, the freedom to be human. And there is broad latitude in that family. When Gloria left home after an argument with Mike and Archie over women's rights, Archie turned to Mike who remained and said, "It looks like we have lost a daughter and gained a meathead." Mike is family.

The decibel level of these shows is high, because they portray basic conflicts over authority and freedom and justice. These conflicts Lear believes to be a "celebration of life."

> They love fiercely, and they bed each other fiercely, and they fight each other on points of view fiercely. And that's life. I don't see a lot of life without conflict. The more interesting lives are led with great and wonderful conflict. It is not possible to exist without it. I like the people who get mad enough to cry and fierce enough to throw things. Caring enough is the same as fierce enough, in the way I mean. And so the shows are peopled with persons who feel that way and express that way. There is room on the tube for lots of . . . passion.

It may be that in reality such strife often leads to family destruction, but Lear would probably assert that a genuine family unit is strong enough to endure.

The TAT shows consistently put forth a strong sense of liberating justice within a generally conservative setting. The idea of social justice is paramount in the series. Yet Lear has room for caring about those who don't see it his way. Concerning Archie, Lear said to me:

> I loved him when he was born because I loved my father who had all of those qualities. I feel it's important to understand that a person who differs from you and is wrong, even a bigot, is lovable because he is a human being and he

must be reached in another way. You can't write him off and hope to reach him.

And Lear is convinced that impact is being made by his presentation. He was quite persuasive when he remarked,

> We do *All in the Family* thinking you can't make a bigot like Archie Bunker look ridiculous week after week after week through all the years without people understanding that that's what you are doing no matter how much some cry to the contrary, "you are reinforcing bigotry."

Edith and, to a greater extent, Mike become the voices of reasoned justice for Archie. According to Al Burton, a TAT executive, Mike is the mouth of Lear. And it is effective to cast such justice against abject bigotry or irrationality, for the result is to make justice appear even more rational.

"And then there's Maude." Lear has said that Maude is the underside of the Bunker narrowness, "a foolish lady liberal." Well, Maude may be foolish, but Archie is the bigot. Maude's folly does not disallow the legitimacy of the positions she espouses. Seldom do Arthur and Vivian carry the Lear message. And while Maude is a "liberal" she possesses numerous "conservative" characteristics. For instance, when her daughter, Carol, arrived home with a man and wished to spend the night with him in Maude's house, she understood as a liberated woman, but as a mother she was shaken and upset.

Maude is honest. When she ran for the New York Senate, she won the hearts of the audience. She told the truth in the face of predicted political disaster. The specter of her political mentor slinking away from her when she dared face an issue honestly should be burned on the retina of every politician who uses words to deceive and fears retribution for his convictions sufficiently to remain silent.

The beautifully conceived two-part drama concerning Walter's alcoholism spoke volumes about human compassion and caring. The hand of Tom Swafford of CBS was in evidence in the final scenes involving the grandchild. Walter had struck Maude in the face. She, trying to help him confront his alcoholism, invited a clergyman, a recovered alcoholic, to come to the home to render assistance. Walter was outraged and ridiculed the thought that he needed help until Carol entered with Phillip to say good-bye.

> Carol: It's hardly the place for a child. I'll pick up the rest of the things tomorrow.
> Phillip: Grampa, I forgot to tell you this morning. I love you a whole lot too!
> Carol: Come on, Phillip. [They leave.]
> Maude: [to Walter] Well, there's only one thing left to do. Go ahead, blacken the other eye.
> Walter: Come on, let's talk, Reverend!

Walter gave up his drinking after facing the crisis of loss of his grandchild. Humor and pathos were laced together for an absorbing story, effectively delineating the serious nature of alcoholism.

One of the most effective ethical statements that has occurred on TV took place in the episodes centered on abortion. In a most morally sensitive TV show Maude and Walter faced a decision on her pregnancy. Carol said to her mother that she should have an abortion. Maude struggled with her feelings, her friends, and her tradition. There was tender sentiment for the unborn child. In the quiet of their bedroom the two adults determined what was right for them. It turned out to be an abortion, but nowhere in the two episodes did either alternative bear the label "wrong." There was no simplistic moralizing, just a cry for freedom and human understanding.

Maude: Listen honey, I was wondering, now that you've had your vasectomy, and if anything happened to me, and you wanted to get married again, and you wanted to be a father again, you couldn't. I mean, have you thought of that Walter?

Walter: I never wanted to become a father before. Why should I want to become one later on?

Maude: I don't understand you, Walter.

Walter: I'm happy to become a father because you want to have a baby, not because I want to become a father. Gin.

Maude: Walter, now what are you trying to do? You picked up two cards and you ginned.

Walter: Now wait a second, Maude. Were you having the baby because you thought I wanted it?

Maude: Well, you do, don't you?

Walter: Sweetheart, would it disappoint you too much to learn that becoming a father was never one of my life's ambitions. I don't know why. For years I used to feel guilty about it. For years people told me I was nuts or selfish. How can I not love kids? Well, I do love kids, but they don't have to be mine. That's probably the worst confession I'll ever make. Do you hate me?

Maude: Of course not, darling. I love you. I love you and I love my life.

Walter: Maude, we have something important to talk about. Gin.

Maude: I take it all back. What are you trying to do to me? I don't even have time to sort my cards and you've ginned out on me.

Walter: Forget the cards, Maude. We have something to talk about.

Maude: What, you decided you want a pickle?

Walter: Maude, I want you to have whatever it is you want. Does that include the baby?

Maude: Well, it did when I thought you wanted it.

Walter: Maude, I think it would be wrong to have a child at our age.

Maude: Oh! So do I, Walter. Oh, Walter, so do I. For other
people it might be fine, but for us, I don't think it would
be fair to anybody. Oh Walter, hold me close.

Walter: Frightened, Maude? About the operation, I mean.

Maude: Oh, don't be ridiculous. Why should I be frightened?
Were you frightened of the vasectomy? I said, were you
frightened of the vasectomy?

Walter: I didn't have it. You see I was psychologically
unprepared. You can ask Arthur. Arthur's a doctor, he told
me . . .

Maude: It's all right. Just tell me that I'm doing the right
thing not having the baby.

Walter: For you, Maude, for me, in the privacy of our lives
you're doing the right thing.

Maude: I love you, Walter Findley.

One of the interesting discoveries in dealing with the
dialogue in the Lear comedies is that the comic lines are
detachable from dramatic themes, which merely reinforces the proposition that Lear is a moralist who conveys
his values and ideas through comedy.

Television will always have need for men and women like
Norman Lear and his associates. Lear is neither savior nor last
great hope. For today, and perhaps tomorrow, his is a voice
reciting words of justice. He and others like him in diverse
professions carry heavy responsibility to contest, to challenge,
to counter the prevailing "wisdom," and it is appropriate to
focus attention now upon others who are doing just that.

M*A*S*H—"PUT A VALUE ON HASHING THINGS OUT!"

M.A.S.H., a show where people are in places of death, is
an extremely funny production. In a setting where the
assigned job is to save lives, there is a heavy imbalance
against the doctors and nurses. The conditions are, as
described by Alan Alda, "weighted in favor of death." The
paradox that allows for utter hilarity in this setting is quite

delicate. A bit too heavy on the war and the humor may become obscene, a bit too light and the characters become "just dippy people at the front." More than any other current series, this one requires constantly deft hands at directing and producing, as well as in the casting. In Gene Reynolds and Larry Gelbart *M.A.S.H.* has had executives to match its extraordinary acting talent, particularly Alda.

M.A.S.H. is not without its critics, who express suspicion because of its too easy humanitarianism cast against all too neat, primitive innocence in an adversary culture. The accusation amounts to a charge of over-simplified solutions to heady problems with the use of sarcastic one-liners. The show could degenerate into just that style, but this has been avoided exceptionally well.

Most people who know or have talked with Alan Alda have discovered him to be delightful and much like the character he plays, Hawkeye. I found him to be a sensitive, highly intelligent, articulate spokesman for quality drama. For him *M.A.S.H.* does possess strong values, but he insists that these values are more than just putting people first. The entire company comes armed with an "unconscious arsenal of feelings" and these are made a part of the end product.

If *Happy Days,* another look back to the fifties, is in the tradition of *Father Knows Best* and *Leave It to Beaver,* *M.A.S.H.* has the lineage of Will Rogers and Mort Sahl. *M.A.S.H.* is history, and we are reminded of this by the allusions to politicians, movies, and sports. The historical setting even blunts some social comment. For instance, while the series is quite strong on antiracism, it is mild on women's rights, and sometimes Hawkeye comes across as a sexual Archie Bunker. Yet with the setting in the fifties, unlike TV of that period, *M.A.S.H.* has many moral assumptions. In fact, *M.A.S.H.* combines the logistics of Korea with many moral issues raised by Vietnam.

Alda believes that TV of the fifties "taught us commercials, life has no bumps, marriage leads to happiness, and stuff like that." While a first look at *M.A.S.H.* might suggest that the quick quip has replaced the "stuff like that," a careful viewing reveals that humor offers few answers, only questions. Alda did not accept the role in *M.A.S.H.* until he made sure it would not become a commercial for the army. "I didn't want to take a position that was neutral to the war." The serious side is never ignored, and the humor must finally submit to the somber nature of the context. When Colonel Henry Blake was written out of the script in the spring of 1975, he was killed while returning to his home in the States. Blake was a bumbling commanding officer who was doing a job required of him. He had no cause except to be himself and to relate to others positively. His death, therefore, was a telling blow. "Why?" inquired Johnny Carson one evening of Alda. The reply was simple and effective. Alda reminded the audience that the show should never get away from the fact that war means death and war takes its toll. The humor in the series must always be subordinate to that reality.

One of the more interesting episodes for examination related to an air force bombardier who had been shot down and was carried to the hospital for care. The combination of too much war and his injury had affected his mind, causing him to claim he was Jesus Christ. The humor extracted from that situation was a combination of slapstick and pathos.

Hawkeye: What's your name soldier?
Bombardier: My name is Jesus Christ.
Hawkeye: Funny, we have a savior by that name.

A CIA agent appeared to question the young man because his claims suggested sinister motives to security people.

Frustrated, the CIA man asked B.J. what we would have if everybody decided they were Jesus. B.J.'s response, "Peace?" At one and the same time, a cheap shot that failed to consider the complexities of the situation and a profound cutting through of all the pointless jargon about loyalty and honor in war. The conclusion? The absurdity of the CIA and war lovers requires exposure through intelligent humor that asks questions.

The religious perspective of the series is humanism. In a recent show Hawkeye was involved in a jeep accident and sustained a severe head injury. Trying to remain conscious until help arrived, he carried on a long monologue before his hosts, a Korean family, none of whom could speak English. Contemplating his hand, Hawkeye wonders at the sophistication of its structure and the marvel of the human thumb. He wonders about its origin. This typifies a religious perspective that seems to be agnostic humanism. Major Frank Burns, on the other hand, is never bothered about such trivia. He is a religious conformist, nearly fanatic. He mouths moralisms while bedding Margaret Houlihan, a highly competent nurse and also a proponent of overt religious propriety. These two actually represent traditional religion rather than Chaplain Mulcahy, a nice fellow, intelligent but naïve. It is, in fact, the chaplain's naïveté that allows him to believe his religious ceremonies have significance in the horror conditions surrounding him. Wearing a ridiculous white straw hat, he plays poker with the men and exudes a kind of calm that is in marked contrast with the rest of the characters. In reality the *M.A.S.H.* group accepts him because he cares, and he respects differences. On one occasion the chaplain's superior appeared for inspection. Obviously an evangelical Protestant, he admonished the Father for his failure to challenge the men to conversion. Mulcahy's commitment to the faith was no less certain and his reactions to the troops who were wounded made a mockery of the visiting superior.

With the demise of Colonel Henry Blake and his fish tackle hat, the cast was joined by Colonel Potter, regular army. Traditions are important to him, but his overwhelming concern is for personnel. He will challenge tradition for them.

On first blush, the healing arts may appear to emerge as the heroic profession. The surgeon has something tangible to offer, his skills to correct severe damage done by war. But just as one looks expectantly to see *M.A.S.H.* awarding semideity to medicine, a soldier dies, surgery fails. The camera freezes on Radar as he contemplates the death of a friend of a few hours for whom surgery was useless. And for a moment the corporal and the captain are united in despair, locked as human beings across a professional chasm. Medicine is a skill, not a charm. At best it repairs what should never have been. And enough doctors put in appearances to demonstrate that the character of medical science is flawed like all human knowledge. What remains are human feelings—respect and self-giving. *M.A.S.H.* "goes rather far sometimes in showing us the way we are."

It is effective war protest but it is much more. It is a call for acceptance. The variety of personalities who populate the show from Klinger to Margaret are accepted as they are. Of course a problem arises when one or more of the characters, like Frank Burns, does not exchange acceptance with his associates. The message is unmistakable, be free and be honest with your fellow creatures. Life should have no dogma save mutual respect one for the other. Since Burns refuses this alternative, being censorious as well as incompetent, he becomes fair game for ridicule and sarcasm in direct proportion to his hypocrisy.

The resulting philosophy is far more than froth. The

points made are strongly humanistic, though usually nontheistic. The show is dogmatic about human freedom, but it makes no pretense to religious roots of the traditional type. Perhaps the character of the chaplain is the clue. In the final analysis it is his calm faith and unshaken, simple belief in people which attracts. His unpretentious faith is a link. We should not wish to make more out of the character than is there; it is, after all, entertainment. Yet, through Mulcahy the series says something profound about genuine religion as the chaplain's private faith expresses itself publicly in nondogmatic form. This may prove disturbing to some religionists who insist that life has no meaning apart from a specific historical divine revelation. *M.A.S.H.* is certainly not the only show to challenge that concept, but it is perhaps the most obvious. This exceptionally well-conceived alternative to traditional dogma, cast in terms of secular humanism, might be an appropriate focus for religious institutions to reexamine their exclusivistic assumptions rather than retreat to the diet of Sunday-morning TV.

There is adrift in the nation a certain feeling of revival of civic piety, coupled with the Bicentennial. The political primaries of the 1976 campaign demonstrated this. Citizens are becoming exercised over moral teachings in the schools, and government officials are responding in larger numbers to calls for prayer. Culture religion, marked by uncritical acceptance of public policy as long as it conforms to bland religious formulas, has demonstrated a singular appeal. Churches and synagogues are tempted to join this hurrah for God and country. Caution is advisable for religious communities, for a more meaningful coalition might be developed with enlightened, socially conscious humanism. One route would be the putting aside of dogma and the extension of overtures to the artistic community of television. This would involve an exhibition of concern for life and justice more than for words, ritual, and form. It would be taking a line from the notebook of Reinhold Niebuhr. Alan Alda believes "there are some people within the industry that have a value system they operate by." This may also be stated of churches.

Unlike the Lear productions, *M.A.S.H.* is a slender reed, somewhat isolated. Threatened by the family hour, it has been salvaged through a transfer to an after-nine spot on Tuesday evening. It will not last forever, but in this dramatic comedy there is the type of programming which sould be eagerly sought by morally sensitive leaders. It raises the appropriate questions for debate and discussion, and for many that is a great deal more than may be said for the modern pulpit.

MTM—A QUIET REVOLUTION

In a 1975 episode of *The Bob Newhart Show,* Bob Hartley was becoming discouraged. A psychologist, he felt the pressure of middle age and little evidence of professional success. In a moment of cogitation he determined to return to his old university and talk to his former major professor concerning his problem. Set to appropriate college music, his visit first elicited unknowing response from the old teacher, beautifully played by Keenan Wynn. Finally, after the old professor recognized his former student, Bob shared his agonies with the now "modish" scholar. Having unburdened himself in all seriousness, Hartley waited for a reply. The professor responded with incredulity, "I thought you knew, it's all a crock."

I have the distinct impression that producer James Brooks of *The Mary Tyler Moore Show* and *Rhoda* might feel inclined to utter these same words were he to be exposed to the large volume of analysis that has recently appeared on the social implications of the character of Mary Richards and her friends who frequent CBS each Saturday evening at nine. As we have noted in another context, Brooks is prone to ask, "Who am I to make social comment?" But the critics move on apace.

Horace Newcomb, a provocative humanistic TV critic, has developed an interesting perspective on *Mary Tyler Moore* which sees the series as an extension of the family concept and therefore a successor to family comedies. He classifies Mary and Rhoda as sisters, Ted Baxter as the adolescent brother, Lou as the father, and Murray as the mother.[3] Later episodes, following Lou's divorce, the departure of Rhoda, and the more frequent appearances of Sue Ann, have tended to discount this scheme, particularly as Mary has matured and Murray has confessed that he was in love with Mary. The Newcomb thesis might be reset to describe the security afforded by office relationships, an alternative to home or family.

A more recent study by James Cheseboro and Caroline Hamsher has an elaborate description of *Mary Tyler Moore* in ethical terms. They see the series as (1) suggesting that "Puritan morality is a viable philosophic system," (2) expressing achievement and success as important values, (3) saying "effort and optimism are always rewarded," (4) proclaiming that "sociability, external conformity, generosity, and consideration for others are appropriate modes of social interaction," and (5) suggesting that "patriotism is an essential spiritual value."[4] This description overtaxes the show. First, the authors do not clearly state what they imply by "Puritan," suggesting that it means honesty. But Puritan morality is far more comprehensive and could hardly be applied to any life-style in the series. Second, it seems that far from being "powerful values to be sought and secured by all," achievement and success are regularly ridiculed as absolute goals. People who have been successful may be respected and glamorous, but these qualities do not apply to the newsroom. And, finally, the patriotism comment lacks support.

Evidence strongly hints that the authors developed a thesis after reading a response to a question by Grant Tinker in *TV Guide*. Tinker said, "The show appears to be rather hip on TV, but in fact she and all the characters in that show—forgetting the comedic characteristics—are all four-square people " (Feb. 16, 1974). [5] Maybe for urban Los Angeles but hardly for Des Moines or Shreveport or Roanoke. These "scholarly" observations miss the mark because they are too elaborate. The show will not bear the weight.

True, Mary Richards is traditional in her sense of personal integrity, what Paula Fass has termed her "decency," [6] but rooted as she is in the Midwest and captive to a code of virtue, Mary is still a modern woman. Moreover, she is a career woman in her mid-thirties, reared in a tradition-filled context which posed the question of her capability to achieve independence. She has learned that she can "cope." While Mary may be "four-square" to Grant Tinker, she is most assuredly a pioneer for vast millions of women over thirty who struggle every day for identity against male dominance and conventionality. Hers was a breath of reasonableness at a time in 1969 when little rationality attached to questions of the female role in society. Mary is every bit a person and every bit a woman. Lou Grant may be wiser, but Mary is smarter, the most intelligently alert individual in the newsroom. One feels that while all the others have reached their level of competence or, in Ted's case, passed it, Mary has not. She is the most capable in dealing with the rising new world that will tend to shatter the sheltered existence of her colleagues. She neither accepts without question past values nor rejects them out of hand. Again, as Paula Fass suggested, Mary has that intangible quality, character. A person with character may successfully crack conventions once she has convinced others that she is genuine. Like the *M.A.S.H.* philosophy, Mary believes, in Brooks's words, "that people should be open and loving towards one another, if that's possible."

Mary Richards has grown in the six years of her life with us. Lately she even addressed Mr. Grant as "Lou." She has been affected by society far more than her compatriots. Mary has enjoyed an active sex life, unrestrained by Puritan mores, yet she has principles that apply to relationships. At least until this year she believed that such relationships should be monogomous, although a recent confrontation may have altered that opinion. Religion, a traditional linchpin in any morality, is almost nonexistent in this show. In the Lear productions religion is often an integral part of the plot, and the producer moves easily with the subject. The MTM works, excepting *Doc,* have tended to shy away from such themes; yet most viewers would see Mary as a product of American Protestant ethics, interpreted through the culture, albeit conditioned by enlightened humanism. Mary is free of dogma and is not judgmental. Her ethics are personal, individual. If Lou's new girl had a "past," it was Mary who insisted that he look at the person she is now. There is a hint that her "past," were it her "present," might be too much to accept.

While in California I had the opportunity to observe the filming of *The Bob Newhart Show.* Producer Jay Tarses answered questions from the audience during breaks in the action. One person asked if the fact that Dr. Hartley's patients were so kooky and never seemed to improve raised ethical issues about the treatment of psychologists.

Without pausing, he responded that this was no problem at all, because the crazier the better. Certainly it would be difficult to disprove that the Newhart wing of the MTM productions is mostly just fun. Issues are neither sought nor obliquely introduced from week to week. The most improbable circumstances prevail for dentists, urologists, and school teachers, not to mention airline navigators. The redeeming social value is a good time.

One would be mistaken, however, if one were to stop with that conclusion. Anyone who has watched Newhart knows that he is a master comedic craftsman. His comedy has generally carried some social freight, and his present show is no exception. A primary matter is, once again, human relations. Persons of various social and ethnic backgrounds appear and relate to the primary characters. Bob and Emily are very much in love. Theirs is a solid monogomous relationship in which even the hint of extramarital sex is missing. They are solid; their marriage is solid. These two middle-aged people have liberal inclinations yet are bound by traditional conventions and mores. They are apartment dwellers, childless, but with the capacity to provide a home setting for the whole cast of characters who frequent the delightful half-hour.

Bob and Emily are advocates of women's rights, which is a regular theme. Bob has trouble with adjustment to this ideological commitment, but he always tries. Emily is uneasy on occasion at expressing her independence; however, she is a remarkably good example of how a generation reared to one way learns to cope when converted to another. The Newhart show is gentle but fair, never harsh in attacking common problems of all viewers.

On several occasions Hartley, as a devotee of sports, has grappled with the problems of athletics and made clear his professional awareness of the devastating effect upon participants. Presented with charm, the dichotomy is nonetheless real. There are no deep recesses in Bob Hartley, just a calm poking of fun at most of the things we know best.

Upon careful observations, *Phyllis* emerges as a characteristically distinguishing mark of MTM in contrast to Lear productions. From *One Day at a Time* to *The Jeffersons* to *Good Times,* the situation, the relationships are the center of attention in Lear's comedies. With MTM, later additions to their offerings have been predicated upon personality. Newhart is distinctive because of his quality as a comedian, and likewise Cloris Leachman and Valerie Harper. For this reason, the mark of the star is far more common at MTM than at TAT. Bea Arthur as Maude comes closest to being the exception at TAT. This quality makes generalizations about MTM much more difficult, if not impossible. In fact, when the question was asked of Jim Brooks about the Newhart show, he responded that he didn't have information. He was concerned with Mary and Rhoda. A conversation with Grant Tinker might lead to understanding of overall intention, but it would almost certainly be far more loose than Lear's.

With *Phyllis* there emerges a teen-ager, Bess, and reality begins to balance MTM comedy. Phyllis, once the most absurd character on Mary's show, became the mother who had to come to terms with reality. Widowed and living with in-laws, Phyllis seems to occupy middle ground, somewhat closer to *One Day at a Time.*

A smashing rating success, *Phyllis* began under a cloud created by CBS censors. I stood in line for two hours before being admitted with my family to a filming of *Phyllis* at CBS headquarters in Los Angeles. The plot concerned Bess who was away for a ski weekend. When her mother called from San Francisco, a boy answered, informing Phyllis that Bess was still sleeping. The rest of the story is predictable. Worried, Phyllis finally decided to confront Bess. Did anything happen with the boy? The scene ended in Bess's bedroom with parent and child in good communication. The trailer showed a contented Phyllis entering the living room where she met her mother-in-law and reported, "Nothing happened!" Then, after an acrobatic leap into the air, she turned and added, "Unless she lied!" That was the grace note.

The public never heard those last three words. Family viewing required excision, and after some debate the producers agreed to the deletion. Those words are a symbol of a raging conflict between creators and network executives. Having been there, I am convinced that the three words spelled the difference between pointless comedy and humor in touch with reality. The stage had been set to make a far more significant point than "Nothing happened!" Phyllis and Bess had grown close to each other in a relationship that was precious enough to mother and daughter that significance of specific events of the weekend faded completely. This incident says that the public will be far better served if the creators make the points rather than the censors.

In all the MTM work there is a lightness, a gentleness, which speaks eloquently to a society such as America. These shows are not about politics or power or patriotism or position; they are about people. Together with *M.A.S.H.* and Lear's productions they compose the best of all television times in comedy.

Chapter VII
No Moral Intended: Of Stars, Sports, and Salaries

Prominent actors have been major subjects of popular interest for centuries. Individuals, identified with playwrights or specific roles, have garnered considerable adulation. But such celebrities have, until recently, depended, primarily, upon a single vehicle (the play) to enhance their notoriety. With the introduction of film there was created what has come to be described as the "star system"—personalities making appeal through the play. The general anonymity of film writers meant that with few exceptions, notable by that fact, the drawing power was transferred to actor or actors. There appears to have been no standard in this new order, so, to enhance the fresh system, Hollywood created a gaggle of sycophants and parasites who produced pulp star magazines and daily newspaper columns. The medium for this star puffery was distinct and separate from the films in which the actors appeared. While the celebrity system worked remarkably well to sell movies and to advance the economic status of a small number of persons who frequented the screen in the thirties, forties, and fifties, promotion of support was dependent, in large measure, upon external media—newspapers, magazines, and later, radio.

Spencer Tracy, Humphrey Bogart, Bette Davis, James Stewart, Ginger Rogers, Cary Grant, Clark Gable became bigger than life and larger, by far, than their movie roles. Meanwhile, radio began to present an entirely new crop of celebrities, many of whom sought and found a place in film. At the same time, radio, through guest appearances, undertook to feed the star consciousness of a responsive public. Radio personalities like Bob Hope, Edgar Bergen, and Jack Benny regularly welcomed "star" guests. The two media were nurturing each other. By early fifties television had discovered an even more incestuous means of promoting the star system.

The marked difference that TV injected into the game was the utilization of a single medium both to package and sell the players. Like the stage, TV tended to return to role players. Chad Everett is Joe Gannon, Richard Thomas is John-Boy, Jim Arness is still Matt Dillon, and Raymond Burr will always be Perry Mason. The weekly reinforcement of character on TV is reminiscent of the Saturday morning movie serials or radio figures like Gildersleeve and Fibber McGee and Molly. The shift in emphasis has not, however, weakened the concept of stardom. The networks have coupled the change with a handy and inexpensive means of star creation. While Johnny Carson's *Tonight Show* has remained a highly successful venture for over a decade, it has been used more and more frequently to promote stars and network series. Actors in new series invariably appear with Carson early in the season to sell their wares. If during these presentations negative review comment is mentioned, it is customary to say, "What do they know?" However, if a critic happens to be complimentary, such as the *Wall Street Journal* was about Carson recently, no less a luminary than John Wayne may appear to commend the late-night host as the subject for a fine column. While Carson, with not inconsiderable talent and humor, may poke fun at the networks, the in-house puffery and self-congratulatory comments are unrelenting. Star appearances in Las Vegas are always catalogued and plugged. Perhaps not always to Carson's liking, his move from New York to Burbank has caused him to become, at times, a semi–press agent.

To a lesser degree, the *Today* show has done a similar job of promotion for NBC. Since the network is commercial, it is quite natural to expect self-advertisement. Because *Today* is partially oriented toward news, it seeks to cloak its interviews with stars in a documentary wrapper.

A variation of this self-promotion on NBC is the Walt Disney enterprise which, for several years, has used its TV time as an expanded commercial for a variety of business ventures.[1] A classic example was the elaborate staging of the grand opening of "Space Mountain" at Disney World in Florida. While the quality of much of Disney's early work was of the highest order, late efforts to promote movies, Florida and California parks, and other endeavors hint at a dimension of TV huckstering that may be ominous.

All three networks conduct elaborate rituals of celebrity promotion on daytime game shows and in syndicated daily interview offerings. During one week in 1976 ninety different show business personalities appeared on seven quiz and interview shows. While a few were currently involved in TV series, 24 percent of the individuals were former TV luminaries and the rest were an assortment of singers and performers in various stages of career incline or decline. But in nearly all cases the emphasis was placed upon "celebrity" status.

Quite obviously promoters and agents are alert to possible means of "puffing" clients. In the past several months the Dean Martin TV appearances have centered around a so-called roast in which personalities are promoted to the public through mock ridicule. On occasion substantial political personalities have participated in these affairs, often with embarrassing results. Television has become a major stage for all types of awards (Emmy, Oscar, Tony), some of which have dubious validity beyond their obvious promotional values. The proliferation of these award shows has begun to suggest problems even to reporters in the industry. Recently Gerry Levin wrote in the *Hollywood Reporter*, "Where is the line of ethics drawn between what can be legitimately called 'awards' and what is simply a gimmick for a TV special?" In this particular instance he had reference to a CBS production entitled "People's Choice Awards" which seemed suspiciously like a sales pitch for one set of products. The most blatant example of the risks of celebrity consciousness has been the protracted negotiations that lured Barbara Walters to ABC News for $1 million per year. Even NBC seems to have become embarrassed over that episode.

While CBS and ABC have made forays into late-night programming of the Carson type, their success has proved minimal. Both networks make use of spot announcements for upcoming programs, but as a rule celebrities take a back seat in these promos.

In the season of 1975-76 ABC introduced a new format entitled *Good Morning, America*, which possesses an interesting formula in contrast with the hard sell of *Today*. This ABC offering is hosted warmly and gently by the actor David Hartman. The intense involvement in his profession which Hartman brought to *The Bold Ones* and *Lucas Tanner* is reflected in his present role. He believes there are definite values which a TV performer can share with his audience, and his humanistic outlook contributes to the strength of *Good Morning, America*. It is, for that reason, a jarring experience to encounter, sandwiched into this new format, the egocentric world of Rona Barrett. With her, the old fan magazine mentality takes to the air with hints of scandal and gossip dripping temptingly from Hollywood. While it is clearly star promotion, Barrett adds a new wrinkle by assuming that she is more important than the menagerie of personalities she discusses.

One of the most convoluted pieces of promotion of self-promotion had prime time on ABC during the fall of 1975. Howard Cossell conducted his own show on Saturday nights as well as acting as commentator on *Monday Night Football*. Alex Karras (now name-dropping in commercials about toilet articles) and Cossell spent time each Monday evening describing the sterling quality of the Cossell Saturday offering, creating the impression of a show within a show. The excessive praise and "humble" obeisance to persons with "great talent" and to "beautiful human beings" was a variation on the fan magazine. It might be observed that ABC did nothing to encourage intelligent viewing by replacing Cossell with *Almost Anything Goes*.

Another cause for concern is the interlocking nature of entertainment stardom and sporting prowess. Golf on TV early traded upon this coalition. Bob Hope, Bing Crosby, Danny Thomas, and Glen Campbell all sponsored golf weekends on television where highly paid athletes competed in a show studded with stars. Exposure is the name of the game, each participant receiving a share, depending upon his score and/or position on the ladder of fame. In these and other events the networks supply coverage by announcers who are, in fact, merely promoters, who with rare exception, puff athletes with reference to their marvelous talent and fine human qualities. The National Basketball Association proclaims, through CBS, prior to each game, that all announcers must have been approved by the NBA.

Sports on TV are monotonously associated with the finest in American patriotism and morality. Some college football coaches have warned, seriously it seems, about the threat of communism, which ideology they believe is most effectively challenged by "amateur" athletics. In the fall of 1975 Tom Brookshire, one of the better announcers, informed his listeners that the quarterback for the Dallas Cowboys was "an incredible American." Well, he may be, but the evidence upon which he based this elaborate opinion seemed to be a strong arm and common decency. For most sports announcers words lose meaning and the superlative is the only degree.

ABC sports coverage, faced with political crisis and tragedy in Munich, resorted to maudlin sentimentality as announcers moralized about the 1972 Olympics, suggesting that such catastrophe might happen elsewhere, but surely should not in the pristine communion of clean-living athletes. Another example of this type of commenting came in the December, 1975, playoff game between Minnesota and Dallas in the National Football Conference. Toward the close of the game, when Dallas had gone ahead, a bottle was thrown from the stands and struck a referee. An announcer piously informed viewers that it was a whiskey bottle, if one wanted to know the truth. It appears that some person, probably drunk from a product massively advertised, had done something quite stupid. The camera switched to the booth where John Unitas proceeded to lecture the nation that such things should not happen in America, perhaps in South America, but not in our beloved land. The capstone came when a third announcer decided to blame the Vikings' quarterback, Fran Tarkenton, because he had argued vehemently with a referee. Somehow this single dangerous act, as reported by sports announcers, had become a symptom of the decline and fall of American morality.

The relation of sports and TV, combined with the exorbitant pay scales of stars, naturally creates a coalition between such activities and other dimensions of the entertainment community. Slowly this money and fame orientation, fed by the potential of instant TV glory, infests college athletics. Some college coaches have become TV celebrities. Other coaches covet the same attention so that high school athletes, thereby attracted to a particular institution, might aid in a winning season. Recruiting of athletes, a vicious practice, becomes more important than good coaching skill. In the "big time" all athletes are given a financial free ride in return for hours of grinding practice and primary commitment to the college team. Since TV is reserved for the successful few, and the money is handsome, there is a mad scramble for the TV dollars. It is anticipated that by 1977 there will be in existence a "major league" of college teams to claim the lion's share of this money. Universities and colleges tend to prostitute academic standards for these benefits. It takes little imagination to see how this disease has crept into high schools and even Little League programs. In the midst of this hysteria, what are the facts? Only 1 percent or less of the athletes who manage through football to a college diploma reach the professional ranks. For untold numbers of the rest of the teen-aged recruits it is a fantasy, marred by pressure and compromise leading to ultimate disappointment. TV money has infiltrated the legitimate aims of education and scholarship. A few alumni have become more significant in some institutions than academic programs. Coaches in reputable schools are heard to say, "Men of letters and lettermen don't mix."

A thoroughgoing investigation of the content of sports programming on television is desperately needed. What role does competition play in the presuppositions of most sports programs? What are the goals of athletics? How often is patriotism equated with athletic prowess? Are American big-time contests true sport? A recent volume by Michael Novak on the subject has provided a defense of sports.[2] An in-depth analysis of the effects and long-range influence of TV sports where moral issues abound remains to be written.

Politics has not escaped the corrosive effects of stardom. By the same token that TV has tempted candidates to be packaged as soap or cereal so also, as Joe McGinniss notes, "It's important, I think, in this new politics to have celebrity identification. It's wrong, but it's important."[3] Politicians since Nixon, Joe McCarthy, Kefauver, and Checkers have spotted the potential. Since variety entertainment on TV is dominated by a celebrity cult, TV political status appears to demand star identification. Recently, Senator Frank Church was on a Democratic Telethon raising funds for his party. He was cast as a TV host, demonstrating an ineptness that could have permanently negated his presidential aspirations. Senator Church is not Johnny Carson or Joey Bishop. If politicians are led by the medium to become such, the electorate may be treated in the future to more and more pseudostatesmen.

Pathetic revelations about Frank Sinatra and President Kennedy, combined with a previously known friendship with Spiro Agnew are a danger signal. Recently a prominent actor defended Sinatra while admitting he knew nothing of the singer's connections. The point was that everyone needs a start, but he must make it on his own after that. Even if that be sufficient for stars of entertainment, it is hardly a satisfactory condition for political leaders. C. Wright Mills made some important comments on these problems two decades ago.

> All those who succeed in America—no matter what their circle of origin or their sphere of action—are likely to become involved in the world of the celebrity.... Based upon nation-wide hierarchies of power and wealth, it is expressed by nation-wide means of mass communication....

The professional celebrity, male and female, is the crowning result of the star system of a society that makes a fetish of competition. In America, this system is carried to the point where a man who can knock a small white ball into a series of holes in the ground with more efficiency and skill than anyone else thereby gains social access to the President of the United States. It is carried to the point where a chattering radio and television entertainer becomes the hunting chum of leading industrial executives, cabinet members, and the higher military. It does not seem to matter what the man is the very best at; so long as he has won out in competition over all others, he is celebrated. Then, a second feature of the star system begins to work: all the stars of any other sphere of endeavor or position are drawn toward the new star and he toward them. The success, the champion, accordingly, is one who mingles freely with other champions to populate the world of the celebrity.[4]

High salary scales, self-adulation, inflated egos, incestuous mutual promotion, are not new with TV, but they are, nonetheless, a distinct problem in the medium. In television the star system functions to limit talent selection and places excessive financial pressures upon producers and directors. The star environment has driven many actors to transcendental meditation or transactional analysis or just plain analysis, creating ancillary star clusters of wealthy analysts and gurus. Even clergymen are measured by their access to presidents, Peale, Graham, for example. Any consideration of the ethical and moral effects of television must grapple with the implications of the massive celebrity system, far more complex than when Mills wrote twenty years ago. The networks could at least begin to attack these problems by paying less to televise "major" sports events, by eliminating star puffery from schedules, and by controlling the personality cult that infests game and variety shows. The talent of Carol Burnett and Johnny Carson do not require these formulas to entertain. Further, the networks could set a ceiling upon salary scales. Many professions have learned the folly of unrestrained pay conditioned upon the old saw "what the traffic will bear." Finally, the citizens should be aware that buyers of goods foot the total bill for a massive rake-off. Harry J. Skornia has documented this in his excellent *Television and Society*.[5]

People appear to need and enjoy heroes and there is no intention here to downgrade this pervasive feeling. From John Smyth to George Washington to Abraham Lincoln to Charles Lindbergh to John Glenn to Stan Musial to Gary Cooper to Fran Tarkenton to Hank Aaron, Americans have found and adored heroes. And, in turn, such figures have claimed certain status in society, appearing bigger than life. They live out the public myths about them. But the recent cancerous growth of a scheme of self-adulation and exploding pay scales threatens to turn the tables. Rather than the public creating its heroes, today's stars tend more and more to develop artificial demand and market for themselves. While this was always possible, the existence of TV has caused a quantum leap in the availability of instant fame.

Rather than stifling creative talent the networks would be better advised to alert themselves to the public interest when the airwaves are bent toward a select celebrity cult.

Chapter VIII
The Future: Electronics and the Family

My analysis of program content on prime-time television unquestionably reflects a positive portrait of the medium and it cannot be gainsaid that the numerous TV producers and actors who manifested both genuine care about their craft and concern over point of view in plot development affected this assessment. Certainly, whether measured by dramatic or more subtle humanistic standards, commercial television has continued to offer an excessive listing of inadequate series. In a group that might include *Bronk*, *The Bionic Woman*, *Harry O*, *S.W.A.T.*, and *On the Rocks*, the last deserves special notice because of its particularly offensive philosophy to the effect that prison can be fun. While any sensitive citizen would desire the state to provide suitable entertainment and pleasure for prison inmates, the presentation of civil confinement as a vaudeville act raises questions of judgment. Yet, granted the present low state of many series, the excessive number of police dramas, the declining quality of many TV movies, and the potential sickness of the celebrity system, I am convinced that for average American viewers in 1977 there is as consistently high a level of entertainment on television as may be experienced in either cinema or legitimate theater. Within that perspective there follows an agenda for change, suggestions for better utilization of existing TV programs, and a final critique and summary.

TV AS MORAL STATEMENT

Whenever the question of ethics and TV arise, religious groups generally bestir themselves as advocates of correc-

The Future: Electronics and the Family

tive action. This usually amounts to negative diatribes against personal "immorality" of the commercial networks for "polluting the airwaves." The chief fault with these often repeated criticisms appears to be the assumption that a particular moral perspective is "the" moral perspective. Perry Miller, in commenting upon the significance of Roger Williams for the American tradition wrote:

> The image of him in conflict with the righteous founders of New England could not be obliterated; all later righteous men would be tormented by it until they learned to accept his basic thesis, that virtue gives them no right to impose on others their own definitions.[1]

Moral outrage is, of course, a common response to those aspects of human activity that are antithetical to one's own heritage and conscience or are outside of one's realm of experience. Every TV viewer brings to the tube a collection of presuppositions and, indeed, the dramas and comedies trade on that fact. A motion picture such as *Rage* assumed a common and pervasive value structure which would create near unanimous response. Similarly, television shows that deal with injustice anticipate an almost universal ethical response. Emotional commitments to freedom and justice along with "traditional" ethical concepts are regularly employed by TV producers and writers to establish long-standing successes, a fact demonstrated by *Bonanza* and *Gunsmoke*.

In order to avoid similar moral assumptions being turned to attack program content of TV, networks have tended toward a consensus morality. "If our society, our culture, offers only relativistic morality, then we can turn on the television set to see problems worked out for us in terms of a simpler set of shared values."[2] While commercially interpreted as safer, imposing such shared values

165

tends to inhibit creativity and, finally, such policy proves unsatisfactory because ethics fluctuate with cultural and religious background. And, ironically, this myth of melting pot morality, traditionally viewed as the "Puritan" ethic, may be turned on its purveyors in highly destructive and restrictive crusades.

In recent months television series have been emboldened to touch more controversial subjects, which have, in turn, elicited more protest and outrage. There is a general failure to understand that one person's heresy is another's faith. Networks and the public alike will be the better when it is determined that the censors' scissors do not provide a satisfactory solution to any complaint.

Groups that parade as voices of conscience for the nation assume a moral superiority often based upon arrogant claims of possessing ultimate truth. Yet the same critic who resents allusions to abortion on *Maude* may support the "old-fashioned virtues" of *Family Affair.* However, that earlier comedy offered, for example, a characterization of Chinese Americans as culturally deprived babes in need of leaning on their native-born American "friends."

Possibly we could live together more comfortably in our multiculture if we established a code for TV which focused on human rights, dignity, and freedom. Such a prohuman, prosocial approach would allow a variety of controversial issues within a context of diversity, and it might have a salutary effect upon TV violence.

Given the present industrial model for commercial television, any proposal dealing with responsibility for programming will require careful delineation. George Gerbner was to the point when he noted that the broadening of TV offerings "can only be done by TV's artists and professionals under arrangements that support rather than distort their own best judgment."[3] Clearly this

166

would result in occasional lapse into poor taste or bad drama, but testing and censorship supply only illusory protection from such lapses. Philip Leacock, supervisory producer of *Hawaii Five-O*, makes this point rather well.

> When you start to do it [control TV content] mechanically, using measuring devices which, I think, are pseudo-scientific, instead of using your own personal good taste, which is all you have as a creative person, then I think you just start getting in a mess. You've got to rely on your own taste in every aspect of this industry. If the public likes it, it's because they like your ideas.... You can't lay down guidelines.

In the long run, we want television content to be determined by no single perspective, be it that of Pat Boone, "Revival Fires," Dean Martin, religious commissions, or Cher.

The broad freedom advocated here may cause initial concern for an ever-increasing number of citizens worried about the influences of television upon their families, especially upon young children. Trading on this concern, one recent ad in *TV Guide* urged parents to join an organization that would promise to supply monthly guides of "the best upcoming programs."

Synagogue and church seem natural institutions to be concerned over TV and children. But effectiveness demands a new, fresh, and positive attitude toward the tube. Father James Brown, former director of Humanitas, has been cited as someone with one such approach.

While viewing habits do vary according to income level and social status, parishioners of most churches watch TV and enjoy it. Yet official church response has all too often been either condemnation of all television offerings on the basis of generalizations about sex and violence or dismissal of TV viewing as a waste of time. Having already commented at length upon the former position, it should prove profitable to examine this second moralistic response to the medium.

Americans need to be relieved of the notion that TV is a waste of time. The heavy burden of the work ethic has been pressed far too hard by many churches. Recreation has required justification. Tennis is good for health; golf helps one lose weight. Relaxation makes for better work habits. Naps are described as recharges for greater concentration. Music relieves tension. Even religion pays dividends, heaven. The insistence that life is primarily work has seldom been challenged in the United States. It is for that reason encouraging to read in Michael Novak's new book that the chief end of life is play (although his focus on American sports may be a poor illustration). And TV is preeminently play, not only in ball games, but in the drama and comedy which populate the evenings. At its very best it may serve, as noted earlier, as an "after-dinner mint."

Suppose, for a change, churches and synagogues stopped listening to the popular wisdom that claims TV to be uncultured and a waste, and began to encourage television watching. A moralizing sermon directed to equal treatment under the law or equal opportunity might be transformed into a vital experience through incorporation of discussion about previously assigned viewing of *Welcome Back, Kotter* or *Good Times.* The interest already exists. By the same token, if adults relax with *Kojak* or *The Waltons,* why not trade upon that interest to create conversation about violence, to stimulate questions on parental relations? A church actively and positively aware of the dimension of family viewing could revolutionize Sunday services. Further, for an investment of less than $5,000 any religious organization could equip a room for recording and displaying TV shows and provide a beginning collection of materials to be viewed and discussed. In most cases only imagination is lacking.

In a recent article by Harlan Hamilton, "TV Tie-Ins as a Bridge to Books," a possible approach to the use of television was developed with a suggestive conclusion.

> In many homes, television is a problem because parents have allowed it to become and remain a problem. In schools, similarly, it may also prove to be a liability when it is ignored. Although many TV programs are mediocre or poor, there are some genuinely informative offerings and occasionally truly inspiring or beautiful presentations. These are surely unrealized possibilities for stimulating appreciation and for fostering worthwhile interests through judicious use of offerings *via* television.[4]

The printing press had much to do with putting the pulpit, with the "Word," at the center of Protestant worship. In 1977 it may be time for at least some churches to heed the musings of my graduate director, Horton Davies, who commented to me in 1956 that one day he hoped to see churches equip their pulpits with consoles elaborate enough to produce instantaneously sound and visual representations integrated into sermons. The orator would be augmented with immediate access to the arts of centuries, the literature and cultures of the world, and the voices of thinkers and doers. Church musicians have proved far more effective at bringing the variety of their art form into living contact with the congregations than have ministers. A brief scene from *Maude* could be a more striking word than a homily on humility. Television, far from replacing religion, could prove to be at least one catalyst for genuine renewal, not of dogma, but of prophetic faith concerned with human dignity, freedom, and justice born out of a context of love and compassion.

Churches and synagogues need to comprehend the

enormous degree to which the American family has included television as an integral family activity. Further, it might be asked, How significant is a half-hour comedy shared by thirty million persons in ten million homes? Religious communities should not bypass this mine of shared experiences out of some false sense of guilt about TV being a waste.

NETWORK TRINOPOLY

In 1972 the three commercial networks had total costs for prime-time entertainment programs of $480 million while program revenues, chiefly advertising, amounted to $800 million. By 1974 total pretax profits for the three networks had risen to $330.8 million, "the highest in broadcasting history."[5] The staggering fact appears to be that no matter what TV fare is offered to the public, profits climb, a condition that will likely continue as long as competition is legally restricted.

For many years there seems to have been a concerted effort on the part of the networks to "encourage" the FCC and Congress to hamper development of cable TV. In January of 1976, President Ford made a statement seemingly sympathetic to cable TV, intended for inclusion in a special issue of the trade paper Broadcasting. The paper made an unfavorable editorial comment about the statement and requested the President to make changes in his submitted remarks. In spite of a staff report of the House Subcommittee on Communications which charged that "the FCC has consistently spoken of the potential of cable television. . . . However, [it] continues to pay only lip-service to such lofty principles while following a protectionist policy,"[6] the Ford administration in March of 1976 issued a statement implying continued support of such protection.

Actually, a policy of the kind described would seem contrary to traditional governmental process by which the infant industry is the one protected from destructive efforts of giant establishments. In the existing capitalist structure, successful TV producers and actors do quite well, but there is a high risk when failures, resulting in enormous losses, far outnumber successes. Conversely, financial risks for networks are small under the wing of the FCC.

The concentration of power which controls creative talent in television is not a great deal different from other similar bureaucratic structures, including those encountered by teachers in academic institutions. For most professors, academic freedom and quality of instruction are primary considerations, no less than is the case in the authentic artistic community in California. For teachers generally, demands to compromise in quality and threats of loss of freedom have become a way of life. Frustration arises from the fact that professors, like directors and producers in television, lack adequate voice in policy decisions. A John Kenneth Galbraith or Norman Lear may develop "clout" sufficient to combat bureaucracy, but for most that is never achieved. In both areas the control of the purse strings lies outside the creative community, which means that the final word on dramatic art may be spoken by a New York executive, just as the final word on academic matters is often spoken by "successful" businessmen, pious clergy, and fund raisers. The scholarly community should be sympathetic with the compromises resulting from network monopoly. For creator, like educator, it's the "only game in town."

For citizens who care about the future of television offerings in the home, protectionism and power imbalance should be causes for alarm. While seeking fundamental change, pressure could be applied to the networks by citizens to alter the ratings system through removal of the link between TV ad rates and audience numbers. As long as advertising costs are pegged to a calculated number of viewers, networks will continue to "counter-program" in efforts to annihilate the offerings, no matter the worth, of the competition. It might be possible to force advertisers to experiment with a spacing of commercials geared to special tastes as an alternative to the broadside method. Suppose ABC and NBC were in competition to achieve excellence rather than profits. A decision to alter rate structure and audience appeal, if adhered to by all three networks, would not likely affect the sum of advertising since the medium would remain attractive for sales. It seems that a fundamental change is called for in which the public interests in the airwaves outweigh margin-of-profit considerations. At present, real variety and multiofferings are stymied by economic practices employed by a defensive trinopoly.

If, even in the present corporate system, the networks would consider alternatives, the TV industry could employ various cultural tastes (or, taste cultures) as criteria for program planning and presentation. Sociologist Herbert Gans insists:

> A good life can be lived by all levels of taste and that the overall taste level of a society is not as significant a criterion for the goodness of that society as the welfare of its members. To put the matter bluntly, neither high culture nor any other taste culture is at present so essential to society's welfare that it requires high priority for public programs.[7]

Historically, of course, TV networks have sought to develop a mass appeal through the beaming of a kind of "overculture" into American homes. Actually, this over-culture was little more than a slice of a taste culture which had been experienced by TV people. Richard Levinson believes, with some justification, that "TV people only know upper middle class." And this may only confirm that in the final analysis there really is no such thing as mass culture, only specific cultural projections made temporarily palatable to a majority through considerable dilution. So while Beaver was for a time acceptable to a large portion of the viewing audience, he really did represent a subculture experienced by a minority. Gans believes there is a solution to be found to this dilemma by encouraging greater diversity and less emphasis on the necessity for mass appeal.

> Instead of the present programming system, which provides content cutting across and thus compromising the standards of several taste publics and serving some not at all, subcultural programming would create for every taste public the specific taste culture which expresses its aesthetic standards. . . . The extent of subcultural specificity would be limited only by the actual existence of publics to be served, and by the financial and other costs of creating culture for a small audience.[8]

This approach is consistent with suggestions being advanced by others, including Michael Novak in his discussions of the "unmeltable ethnics." It is in marked contrast with the more traditional "intellectual" argument which rejects TV as being culturally bankrupt. Many persons in literature and the arts have charged the medium with dereliction of responsibility toward what Gans calls "high culture." Martin Mayer believes some of that hostility toward TV "is motivated by the critics' desire to keep lesser breeds from having too good a time."[9]

Most observers agree that the search for an elusive mass culture is fruitless, and efforts to create one are doomed. The nation is no melting pot and there is no single prevailing moral code. Any attempt to enforce one would be arbitrary and capricious. Myopic demands for specific cultural morality in media are logical extensions of efforts at establishing a mass taste. Of course, some less subtle values typical of an American political tradition have filtered through historical experiences—justice, freedom, equality, fairness, happiness. However, protection of even these basic ingredients of our constitutional democracy depends on nondogmatic good judgment. As an open society, we must rely, as in the past, upon true artists using the current artistic media to express ideas, to expound values, and even to err.

I believe that the Gans approach needs modification because recognition of the richness and diversity of cultures does not necessitate totally isolated presentations to ever smaller subcultural units. I cannot agree with him that *All in the Family* is patronizing to the work class, if indeed there is a "work class" in America. It would be a mistake for creators to focus so narrowly as to totally "work for and in a specific taste culture." We have yet to see what a community of craftsmen might do if freed from censorship and encouraged by new policies from the FCC respecting cable TV and expanded numbers of VHF channels. Greater emphasis upon specific taste cultures does not demand total fragmentation.

Finally, some attention should be directed toward a tendency to lump all TV together without differentiation. This demeans even the quality now available from the three networks. Just because there appears at present to be an insistence on the part of networks that programming be controlled by a philosophy of mass culture, it does not follow that all talent in production and acting are reduced to a common level. Existing excellence should be credited, something not achieved by oversimplified generalizations. A list of names that includes Hawkins,

174

The Future: Electronics and the Family

Leacock, Hamner, Lear, Gelbart, O'Brien, Victor, Reynolds, Glicksman, Tinker, and Mann suggests something other than unrelenting mediocrity. Of course, TV drama could be better, comedy more effective, but brickbats accomplish little. Norman Lear made a most interesting observation about the TV industry in comparison with its modern counterparts during a discussion in the summer of 1975.

> I don't think the television industry is so much different than the rest of American industry and government. As a matter of fact, I think in some ways they do a better job. I would put them up against the three top motor car companies in this country anytime—what motor companies in this country have delivered to us in terms of safety and economy and all the things they should be caring about; against the oil companies; against the last three administrations. Television doesn't look so bad when you compare the three networks in that way.

TV is real, it is a quarter-century old, and it is a massive contributor to society. As a technological marvel it will be bent to serve those who discover effective ways to put it to use.

THE TV CRITIC

As with any public medium, television is justifiably a target for competent and responsible criticism. Because movies, plays, art, music, and literature are usually singular, critics in these areas have established neat and accepted guidelines. The nature and scope of television criticism is altogether different, demanding new forms. Questions as to who should, for instance, review a documentary and on what basis, create considerable agony. A presentation on a foreign policy issue might be effective drama and bad history. Depending upon the criteria for the review and the expertise of the reviewer, results could be markedly affected. Or again, which of the twenty-odd episodes of a TV series should be considered by a reviewer? The competent television critic is frustrated by a mammoth task, for there seems no end either to the programming or its diversity. Good, solid writers like John O'Connor and John Leonard of the *New York Times*, Cleveland Amory of *TV Guide*, and Steve Scheuer of *TV Key* recognize limitations and do indeed function remarkably well in a new discipline in spite of handicaps. Still, outside major metropolitan areas, TV criticism remains largely an uncharted profession.

Some organized efforts to examine the role of the critic by groups concerned about the humanities have recently emerged, including two volumes published by the Aspen Institute's Program on Communications and Society. It may be hoped that community by community, newspapers will become aware of the importance of assigning competent and qualified critics to cover television, persons who may perceive their task as a career established as certainly as that of movie or theater critic.

VIOLENCE AND THE SCHOLAR AS CRITIC

While the best newspaper critics have sought to deal constructively with daily offerings on the tube, there has arisen a second order of critical analysis that threatens some distortion of the medium. Literally hundreds of articles by scholars have been published, most of them having concentrated on the subject of violence. "Scientific" studies of television's effect which have bubbled forth over the past two decades have dealt largely with TV in an artificial laboratory setting. In few instances was the environment of normal television watching reproduced. While the subject of violence has received detailed

176

treatment in a previous chapter, a further comment in the form of a summary seems appropriate.

In most of the violence studies, few references have been made to specific TV programs. Individual episodes are usually absorbed in generalizations about "violence-filled programs," "people who watch a lot of TV," "TV's symbolic world of violence." In a current article for *Psychology Today*, George Gerbner and Leonard Gross employ all these phrases, with not one mention of a specific series. The consequent blurring together of shows like *Police Story* and *S.W.A.T.*, *Good Times* and *Almost Anything Goes* seems irresponsible, particularly so when appearing under the title "The Scary World of TV's Heavy Viewer." Gerbner and Gross are undoubtedly correct in saying that "the effect of TV should be measured not just in terms of immediate change in behavior, but also by the extent to which it cultivates certain views of life." [10] Such measurement, however, remains extremely difficult as long as content analysis is quantified and little apparent attention is devoted to individual differences in programming.

While discussions of this type might normally be relegated to friendly debate among professors, the very public nature of every tidbit of scholarly inquiry into television eliminates that possibility. When Gerbner issued his "violence index," banner headlines proclaimed "No Dip Reported in TV Violence." [11] In most newspapers the public was not informed about the nature of the index, only that the late Congressman Torbert MacDonald was disturbed at the results. Immediately CBS branded the Gerbner report "fallacious." Scholarship, politics, and business were intertwined, making understanding difficult for the majority of citizens.

I have argued in this book that the question of violence cannot be separated from the individual programs being observed. It seems fundamental to me that violent scenes on a segment of *Police Story* called "Little Boy Lost" may in no way be equated with violent acts exploited on *The Rockford Files*. In fact, some episodes of the same series may be impossible to compare because of the peculiar nature of individual plots. As noted earlier, Shakespeare included violence, but is it legitimate to allow those classic dramas to be compared, violent act by violent act, with a *S.W.A.T.* plot? One-to-one correlations of different violent acts are not very informative and border upon being unwise misdirection of the public.

For adults, television appears to be primarily a medium of reinforcement, capable of altering images of external reality, but of little significance relative to ideological changes. TV sells products by associating them with presumed viewer values. It is far less clear how TV has been affecting basic ideas of children, but to isolate the effects of television, programs and ads, from the countless other influences on a child's development is, I believe, impossible. Over the past thirty years Americans have experienced the trauma of atomic weaponry, an emotion draining cold war with Russia and China, the threat of McCarthyism, the fear of Dulles brinkmanship, the misery of Korea, the Bay of Pigs, Berlin, Hungary, the panic of Sputnik, the horrors of Dallas, Memphis, and Los Angeles, the deceit of Vietnam, the chaos of Chicago, the crises of Pentagon Papers, Presidential impeachment and dishonor, Agnew, the Byzantine mysteries of the CIA and FBI, and the destructiveness of drugs. Does anyone seriously dare make judgment as to the independent effects of TV violence?

An interesting illustration of the problem laboratory research generates may be found in a 1972 study by four scholars who concluded "that young adult's aggressiveness is positively related to his preference for violent television when he was 8-9 years old and, furthermore, that his preference for violent television during this critical period is one cause of his aggressiveness." [12] Now stand back from that sentence. What does it say? It asserts that aggression-prone children watch violent TV and that these same subjects are likely to be aggression-prone adolescents. The study merely informs us that aggressive people tend to stay that way and that they tend to like violence on TV. The questioners seem not to have asked the obvious, but possibly unanswerable, prior question, "What caused the aggression which caused the preference for violent TV?"

The danger point in TV violence seems to lie in its capacity to reinforce cultural patterns already established. A continued massive reinforcement of violence could result in stagnation of cultural evolution and change. Preliminary indications suggest a possible trend toward a slight diminution of violence in series during 1976-77, but forecasting for such a fast-moving industry would be folly.

In sum, the rhetoric over this subject has been itself violent and dogmatic, leading to some unhealthy and uninformed conclusions. A clearer understanding of terms is needed in discussions of the entire subject of violence. Many so-called violent series are far from antisocial and some of the most effective prosocial incidents have occurred in plays containing violence. Conversely, we have shown there are numerous instances of gratuitous violence, physical and mental. There has been, as Alan Alda indicated effectively, a failure to deal with the consequences of violence affecting all the victims of a single violent act. Further, all too often in recent months, romanticized scripts have suggested that competition, generally violent, is the only effective means to achievement. For these reasons, context and plot, intent and audience, are key considerations that must be weighed in any search for accurate descriptions of violence content and impact.

TV SERIES VS. MOVIES

While, as a rule, series violence is restrained in order to avoid negative response to a weekly hero, the same cannot be said for the growing number of movies, many made for TV, that are populating the airwaves. Sheer sensationalism may not be the only motivation in movies that are being produced for TV; nevertheless, they are a quantum leap from TV series. As the number of TV movies grows, the audiences should be aware that gratuitous violence and bad taste are more easily incorporated with little financial risk. The fear of negative reputation which might attach to a series does not apply to most movies. Each is distinct and singular. Anonymous writers and producers can escape a large measure of that self-imposed accountability described in the earlier remarks from Philip Leacock.

Unfortunately, if violent extremes appear in TV movies and there is sizable audience response of a positive nature, the networks will be listening. If the local cinema were to co-opt the tube, an entirely new situation would prevail. This book has been based upon an assumption of the continuation, at least for the foreseeable future, of a series format for television. Until such time as far more channels are made available outside the major cities, a reduction of such series could have devastating impact. Most Americans are unaware that television has created a rather unique and interesting dramatic form, one that after twenty-five years is in a continuing process of experimentation. Dramatic and comedy series, nevertheless, appear to be on the road to maturity and concerned viewers would do well to encourage constructive criticism leading to more rapid improvement of what it is proper to describe as a highly personal format. Kojak and Marcus Welby have earned visiting rights in many homes whose inhabitants would be loathe to grant the same privilege to Charles Bronson or Clint Eastwood. Commercial networks, dominated by movies, would be a major new departure with serious implications.

SOME EXCLUSIONS AND A CONCLUSION

Due to the nature of the present undertaking, some areas of television have gone unmentioned. Perhaps the most obvious omission from a book on ethics is that of Saturday morning programming which has gone through major changes in the past several years. What has been substituted for cartoon mayhem appears to be poorly acted and of questionable worth. Grotesque caricatures of the Muppets abound and morals are everywhere. Whether this has proved salutary to child viewers is a matter for further investigation. Again, no serious attention has been focused upon advertising and its appeal to public emotions. Ads work, and until an alternative source of funds is discovered, the advertiser remains the lifeblood of the industry. Nevertheless, most ads are offensive and obtrusive, interrupting lines of thought and demonstrating a monumental lack of imagination and taste. Values are unrelentingly pressed, not the least of which is to consume, consume, literally, at all cost. Oil companies spend millions to propagandize for an industry position, not to sell a particular brand. Other manufacturers do the same. Children learn at an early age that adults on TV cannot be trusted. Why? Ads encourage the purchase of toys which either do not operate or break easily. False advertising turns many a child cynical long before he is prepared to cope with the meaning of the experience. Ads are sexist, racist, *and* effective tools of sales. The means to cope with this phenomenon is the subject for further study and its absence from these pages in no way indicates a lack of serious concern for that which consumes nearly one quarter of viewing time in any hour.

Finally, a word about news programs and documentaries. These are a study in themselves and some creative thought has been focused on them recently by David Halberstam and Michael Robinson.[13]

TV still has a great deal of catching up to do. Women are still largely stereotyped; persons over sixty-five are the subject of repetitive and obnoxious humor; ethnic minorities are often ignored or relegated to TV comedy; few blacks have been sought in dramatic roles. The list is long, but it is no more than a reflection of our existing society. Television has been timid, and it has a strong tendency to ignore its own significance in the national life.[14]

Continual viewing over long periods has convinced me that television consistently, in the prime-time hours of network series, presents a reasonably conforming image of our society. Overall, the image is one of hope and positive values, coupled with strong emphasis upon law and order. The picket fences have gone, but the style lingers in numerous ways. TV is a conserver.

Yet this conserving tendency is more and more balanced with a maturing of comedy and drama. It is not the return of the "golden age" but the growth of that alternative style adopted in the early sixties. Comedy has risen to fine levels in the past five years thanks in large part to Tinker and Lear and Gelbart. Police drama has begun to come of age. *Kojak* has introduced a valid dimension of ethnicity into a strikingly well-produced series. *Police Story* continues to demonstrate that law and order can entertain, educate, and proclaim values all at once, without pretense.

If TV creators have the imagination to combine the personal nature of the medium with its potential for conveying ideas and values through entertainment, television may emerge as a bridge linking the traditional nuclear family with changing and growing cultures, society, and politics. Supplying evidence for this possibility has been a primary motivation for this book.

Notes

Introduction

1. Herbert I. Schiller, *The Mind Managers*, p. 84.
2. Among those works of particular interest see Erik Barnouw, *Tube of Plenty*; Horace Newcomb, *TV: The Most Popular Art*; Muriel Cantor, *The Hollywood Television Producer*; Les Brown, *Television, The Business Behind the Box*; David Halberstam, "CBS: The Network and the News & The Power and the Profits," *The Atlantic Monthly*, January and February, 1976.
3. Richard M. Hunt, "No-Fault Guilt-Free History," *New York Times*, 16 February 1976, 19:2.

Chapter I

1. *New York Times*, 23 January 1926, 10:5.
2. *New York Times*, 20 April 1927, 30:2.
3. Sydney W. Head, *Broadcasting in America*, pp. 149-50.
4. *London Daily Mail Year Book*, 1931.
5. *New York Times*, 15 February 1950, 50:6.
6. Martin Mayer, *About Television* (New York: Harper & Row, 1972), p. 398.
7. TV Criticism Conference sponsored by Aspen Institute on Communications and Society, July 26-31, 1975. By invitation of the Institute I was a participant in the Conference.
8. Muriel Cantor, *The Hollywood Television Producer*, p. 6.
9. Hubbell Robinson, Jr., "The Hatchet Men," *Saturday Review*, 14 March 1959, p. 56.
10. "Why Johnny Can't Write," *Newsweek*, 8 December 1975, p. 60. See also a highly suggestive article in *TV Guide*, 4 September 1976, p. 6, entitled "How Television Helps Johnny Read," by Max Gunther.
11. Neil Postman, "Illiteracy in America: Position Papers—The Politics of Reading," *Harvard Educational Review*, 40, May 1970, p. 249.

Chapter II

1. See Muriel Cantor, *The Hollywood Television Producer*.
2. "Playboy Interview: Norman Lear," *Playboy*, March 1976, p. 58.

Chapter III

1. Erik Barnouw, *Tube of Plenty*, pp. 163-65.
2. These words of Chairman Wood's are taken from the Congressional Hearings of the Committee on Un-American Activities, as quoted on the play program for Eric Bentley's *Are You Now, Or Have You Ever Been . . . ?* presented in 1975 at the Ford Theater, Washington, D.C.

3. David Halberstam, "CBS: The Power and the Profits," *The Atlantic Monthly*, January, 1976, pp. 46-47.
4. *Variety*, 7 January 1976, p. 103.
5. Arthur Shulman and Roger Youman, *The Television Years*, p. 294.
6. Federal Communications Commission, "Report on the Broadcast of Violent, Indecent and Obscene Material," 19 February 1975.
7. Letter from Torbert H. MacDonald, Congressman, Chairman, Subcommittee on Communications, to Richard Wiley, Chairman, FCC, November 20, 1975.
8. See Torbert MacDonald," 'Family' Rules a Classic Case," *Variety*, 7 January 1976, p. 103.
9. "What's Happening to American Morality?" *U.S. News and World Report*, 13 October 1975, p. 40.
10. *Ibid., p. 40.*
11. *Duke K. McCall, "Thinking Aloud," The Tie*, October, 1975, p. 15.
12. See *Variety*, 6 January 1976, p. 103, for series rating averages.
13. Neil Hickey, "Does America Want Family Viewing Time?" *TV Guide*, December 6-12, 1975, pp. 4-8.
14. Letter from Virginia Carter to Norman Lear, January 5, 1976, re: Dr. Christie's evaluation of *TV Guide* article as relayed to Carter.

Chapter IV

1. *New York Times*, 15 September 1954, 48:3.
2. *New York Times*, 25 May 1956, 47:5.
3. Peter Schrag, "The Great American Swashbucklers," *More*, November 1975.
4. By contrast, in a 1972 episode on abortion, Dr. Welby approaches this issue neither moralistically nor legalistically. For the pragmatic Marcus Welby, the welfare of his patient and her psychological state determine his decision. He can express respect for the attitudes of the girl's parents, while deploring "parental tyranny."
5. James M. McLaughlin, "Characteristics and Symbolic Functions of Fictional Televised Medical Professionals and Their Effect on Children" (M.A. diss., The Annenberg School of Communications, University of Pennsylvania, 1975), p. 10. This research did not include the most recent programs, *Medical Story* and *Doctors' Hospital*.
6. Dialogue in this chapter was taken from program airings.
7. Michael Novak, "Television Shapes the Soul," *Television as a Social Force: New Approaches to TV Criticism*, ed. Richard Adler, p. 21.

Notes

8. McLaughlin, "Fictional Televised Medical Professionals," p. 36.
9. Cleveland Amory, "Review," *TV Guide*, November 1-7, 1975, p. 20.
10. *New York Times*, 20 January 1976, Sec. 1, p. 1.

Chapter V

1. Hilde T. Himmelweit, *Television and the Child*, p. 220.
2. *Television and Growing Up: The Impact of Televised Violence*, Report to the Surgeon General, United States Public Health Service. From the Surgeon General's Scientific Advisory Committee on Television and Social Behavior. U.S. Government Printing Office, Washington, D.C., 1972, pp. 11-13. This volume is one of a series of six which document government-sponsored research concerning television. The six volumes together are referred to as *Television and Social Behavior*.
3. See Leonard Eron, Monroe Lefkowitz, L. R. Huesmann, L. O. Walder, "Does Television Violence Cause Aggression?" *American Psychologist*, April 1972, p. 253.
4. Herbert Gans, *Popular Culture and High Culture*, p. 32.
5. George Comstock *et. al., Television and Human Behavior: The Key Studies*, p. 155. Commenting upon the Gerbner index of violence, the study notes, "there is always the possibility that the existence of an index will lead to policy decisions and corrective measures in the absence of any evidence that what is reflected in the measure is in any way harmful."
6. George Gerbner, "Scenario for Violence," *Human Behavior*, October 1975, p. 69.
7. Surgeon General's report, *Television and Growing Up*, p. 76.
8. *The Case Against Capital Punishment*, published by the American Civil Liberties Union, 1968, Exhibit 12.
9. *The Bold Ones* had for a brief period a segment that combined the work of a police officer and a district attorney.
10. Himmelweit, *Television and the Child*, p. 178.
11. Horace Newcomb, *TV: The Most Popular Art*, p. 90.
12. James Cheseboro and Caroline Hamsher, "Communication, Values, and Popular Television Series," in *Television: The Critical View*, ed. Horace Newcomb, p. 21.
13. Benjamin Stein, "Keep Winning, Kojak—for Society's Sake," *TV Guide*, May 17-23, 1975, pp. A-5.
14. This, and all script dialogue, is taken from actual broadcasts.
15. Michael Novak, "Television Shapes the Soul," *Television as a Social Force: New Approaches to TV Criticism*, p. 14.

16. Surgeon General's report, Television and Growing Up, pp. 170-71.
17. Ibid., p. 170.
18. "NBC Sets Sights Wide for '76-'77," The Hollywood Reporter, 20 January 1976, p. 1; "Comedy Still King at CBS as 1976-77 Pilots Are Set," The Hollywood Reporter, 22 January 1976, p. 1.
19. James A. Brown, "The Professor's View," in James A. Brown and Ward L. Quaal, Broadcast Management: Radio and Television (New York: Hastings House, 1975), pp. 439-40.
20. Los Angeles Times, 23 July 1975.
21. From scripts for "The Breakdown," "The Sermon," and "The Genius," all supplied by Earl Hamner.

Chapter VI

1. Spencer Marsh, God, Man, and Archie Bunker, p. 22.
2. Neil Vidmar and Milton Rokeach, "Archie Bunker's Bigotry," Journal of Communication, 1974, p. 47.
3. Horace Newcomb, TV: The Most Popular Art, pp. 51-54. This is an excellent book. Newcomb has come at the TV question as a practicing member of the humanities and the results are gratifying. A volume that should receive a good deal more attention than it seems to have so far.
4. James Cheseboro and Caroline Hamsher, "Communication, Values, and Popular Television Series," in Television: The Critical View, ed. Horace Newcomb, pp. 14-16.
5. Ibid., p. 7.
6. Paula Fass, "Television as Cultural Document: Promises and Problems," Television as a Cultural Force, ed. Richard Adler, p. 42. An absolutely first-rate analysis by a historian.

Chapter VII

1. Herbert Schiller, The Mind Managers, pp. 94-103.
2. Michael Novak's The Joy of Sports (New York: Basic, 1976) is a most stimulating defense of a "mythic world" as he terms it. It calls for thoughtful reading and forceful response.
3. The quote is from a taped interview held with Joe McGinniss in Chicago and distributed through The Center for Cassette Studies, Inc., Hollywood, CA. See also The Selling of the President, 1968.
4. C. Wright Mills, The Power Elite, pp. 71, 74.
5. This is an excellent analysis of the industry, though written in 1965. It is somewhat dated and reflects some of the sixties' penchant for putting down the medium. Nevertheless, a pioneering effort that should not be ignored.

Notes

Chapter VIII

1. Perry Miller, *Roger Williams* (New York: Atheneum, 1962), p. 254.
2. Horace Newcomb, *TV: The Most Popular Art*, p. 133.
3. George Gerbner, "Scenario for Violence," *Human Behavior*, October 1975, p. 69.
4. Harlan Hamilton, "TV Tie-Ins As a Bridge to Books," *Learning Arts*, February 1976, p. 130. In the *TV Guide* issue for May 1-7, 1976, Louise Bates Ames of the Gesell Institute of Child Development advised parents not to complain about TV, rather use it. She closed her excellent remarks with the following comment: "If parents show respect for, or at least interest in, their teen-agers' favorite programs, useful and interesting discussion can often be stimulated. There is nothing more important to a 15-year-old than to have somebody listen to and respect his opinions whether agreeing with him or not. Situations and values shown on the television screen can be used as topics for lively and productive discussion." Louise Bates Ames, "Don't Complain About TV—Use It," *TV Guide*, May 1-7, 1976, p. 4.
5. Alan Pearce, "The Television Networks," a paper presented at the 1975 National Conference of Black Lawyers Convention, October 30–November 2, 1975, pp. 13, 16 of typed manuscript, supplied by the author.
6. "House Report on Cable and Commercial TV," *Variety*, 28 January 1976, p. 38.
7. Herbert Gans, *Popular Culture and High Culture*, p. 130.
8. *Ibid.*, p. 133.
9. Martin Mayer, *About Television*, p. 398.
10. George Gerbner and Leonard Gross, "The Scary World of TV's Heavy Viewer," *Psychology Today*, April 1976, p. 45.
11. *Richmond Times Dispatch*, 2 April 1976.
12. Leonard Eron, Monroe Lefkowitz, L. R. Huesmann, L. O. Walder, "Does Television Violence Cause Aggression?" *American Psychologist*, April 1972, p. 253.
13. David Halberstam, "CBS: The Network and the News," The *Atlantic Monthly*, January and February 1976; Michael Robinson, "American Political Legitimacy in an Era of Electronic Journalism," *Television as a Social Force.*
14. Kevin Phillips, "News Watch," *TV Guide*, March 27–April 2, 1976, pp. A-3.

Bibliography

Adler, Richard, ed. *Television as a Social Force: New Approaches to TV Criticism.* New York: Praeger, 1975.
————. *Television as a Cultural Force.* New York: Praeger, 1976. This study and the previous one are sponsored by the Aspen Institute for Humanistic Studies.
Alley, Robert S., writer and producer. *Television: For Better or For Worse.* Thirty-minute film on values and television available through WCVE TV, Richmond, Virginia, 1976.
Arlen, Michael J. *Living-Room War.* New York: Tower Publications, 1971.
Barnouw, Erik. *Tube of Plenty: The Evolution of American Television.* New York: Oxford University Press, 1975. Barrett, Marvin, ed. *Moments of Truth.* New York: T. Y. Crowell, 1975. This is the fifth Alfred I. duPont-Columbia University Survey of Broadcast Journalism.
Blumler, Jay G. and McQuail, Denis. *Television in Politics: Its Uses and Influences.* Chicago: University of Chicago Press, 1969.
Brown, Les. *Television: The Business Behind the Box.* New York: Harcourt, Brace, Jovanovich, 1971.
Cantor, Muriel G. *The Hollywood Television Producer.* New York: Basic Books, 1972.
Cole, Barry G. *Television: A Selection of Readings from TV Guide Magazine.* New York: The Free Press, 1970.
Comstock, George. *Television and Human Behavior: The Key Studies.* 3 vols. Santa Monica, CA.: The The Rand Corporation, 1975.
Elliott, William Y., ed. *Television's Impact on American Culture.* East Lansing, MI.: Michigan State University Press, 1957.
Epstein, Edward J. *News from Nowhere: Television and the News.* New York: Random House, Vintage Books, 1973.
Friendly, Fred W. *Due to Circumstances Beyond Our Control* . . . New York: Vintage Books, 1968.
Gans, Herbert J. *Popular Culture and High Culture.* New York: Basic Books, 1975.
Grant, Gurney Wingate, II. "The Family Viewing Concept: A Content Analysis." Master's thesis, University of North Carolina, 1976.
Groombridge, Brian, *Television and The People.* Middlesex, England: Penguin, 1972.
Head, Sydney W. *Broadcasting in America.* 2nd ed. Boston: Houghton Mifflin, 1972.
Himmelweit, Hilde T., Oppenheim, A. N., and Vince, Pamela. *Television*

Bibliography

and the Child: An Empirical Study of the Effect of Television on the Young. 2nd ed. London: Oxford University Press, 1962.

Kaye, Evelyn. *The Family Guide to Children's Television: What to Watch, What to Miss, What to Change and How to Do It.* New York: Pantheon Books, 1974.

Marsh, Spencer. *God, Man, and Archie Bunker.* New York: Harper and Row, 1975.

Mayer, Martin. *About Television.* New York: Harper and Row, 1972.

McGinniss, Joe. *The Selling of the President, 1968.* New York: Simon & Schuster; Pocket Books, 1972.

McLuhan, Marshall. *Understanding Media: The Extensions of Man.* New York: McGraw Hill, 1964.

Melody, William. *Children's Television: Economics of Exploitation.* New Haven: Yale University Press, 1973.

Metz, Robert. *CBS: Reflections in a Bloodshot Eye.* Chicago: Playboy Press, 1975.

Mickelson, Sig. *The Electric Mirror: Politics in an Age of Television.* New York: Dodd, Mead, 1972.

Mills, C. Wright. *The Power Elite.* New York: Oxford University Press, 1959.

Minow, Newton, Martin, John B., and Mitchell, Lee M. *Presidential Television: A Twentieth Century Fund Report.* New York: Basic Books, 1973.

Newcomb, Horace, ed. *Television: The Critical View.* New York: Oxford University Press, 1976.

Newcomb, Horace. *TV: The Most Popular Art.* New York: Anchor Press, 1974.

Noll, Roger G., Peck, Merton J., and McGowan, John J. *Economic Aspects of Television Regulation.* Washington: Brookings Institution, 1973.

Owen, Bruce M., Beebe, Jack H., and Manning, Willard G. *Television Economics.* Lexington, Mass.: D. C. Heath, Lexington Books, 1974.

Schiller, Herbert I. *The Mind Managers.* Boston: Beacon Press, 1974.

Schramm, Wilbur. *Mass Media and National Development: The Role of Information in the Developing Countries.* Stanford: Stanford University Press, 1964.

Schwartz, Tony. *The Responsive Chord.* New York: Anchor Press, 1974.

Shanks, Bob. *The Cool Fire: Television and How to Make It.* New York: W. W. Norton, 1976.

Shulman, Arthur and Youman, Roger. *The Television Years.* New York: Popular Library, 1973.

Skornia, Harry J. *Television and Society: An Inquest and Agenda for Improvement.* New York: McGraw-Hill, 1965.

Stein, M. L. *Shaping The News: How the Media Functions in Today's World.* New York: Washington Square Press, 1974.

"A Study of Messages Received by Children Who Viewed an Episode of 'Fat Albert and the Cosby Kids.'" Office of Social Research, CBS/Broadcast Group, 1974.

Television and Social Behavior. 6 vols., Report of the Surgeon General's Scientific Advisory Committee on Television and Social Behavior, 1972.